KT-485-053

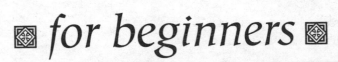

I CHING
for beginners

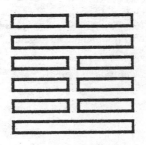

KRISTYNA ARCARTI

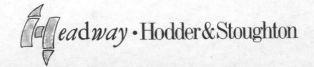

Headway · Hodder & Stoughton

With sincere thanks to John and Darren for their selfless help and support, and to Zoe and Carole for their friendship

The publishers would like to thank Penguin Books for permission to use material from *The I Ching or Book of Changes*, rendered into English by Cary F. Baynes (Arkana 1989, first published by Routledge and Kegan Paul Ltd.) copyright © Bollingen Foundation Inc. 1950, 1967.

British Library Cataloguing in Publication Data

Arcarti, Kristyna
  I Ching for Beginners
  I. Title
  133.33

ISBN 0–340–62080–3

First published 1994
Impression number   10 9 8 7 6 5 4 3 2 1
Year   1999 1998 1997 1996 1995 1994

Copyright © Kristyna Arcarti

All rights reserved. No part of this publication may be reproduced or transmitted in any form or by any means, electronic or mechanical, including photocopy, recording, or any information storage and retrieval system, without permission in writing from the publisher or under licence from the Copyright Licensing Agency Limited. Further details of such licences (for reprographic reproduction) may be obtained from the Copyright Licensing Agency Limited, of 90 Tottenham Court Road, London W1P 9HE.

Typeset by Wearset, Boldon, Tyne and Wear.
Printed in Great Britain for Hodder & Stoughton Educational, a division of Hodder Headline Plc, 338 Euston Road, London NW1 3BH by Cox & Wyman Ltd, Reading.

CONTENTS

INTRODUCTION

What is I Ching?

To many, I Ching, also known as the Book of Changes, is a means of obtaining advice and answers to questions of importance. However, I Ching does not stop there: it also provides a wealth of beautiful poetry and oriental philosophy.

The Book of Changes is at least 5000 years old, and is one of the oldest and most spiritual books in the world. To the Chinese it is one of the five sacred classics, and it commands a special place in the hearts of the people. To many Chinese, it is as important as the Bible is to Western society. Unlike the Bible, however, it is not meant to be read straight through.

Many people from both East and West consult the Book of Changes regularly for help and advice, just as others have done for thousands of years.

The Book of Changes

Chinese legend suggests that, about 5000 years ago, the first Chinese Emperor Fu Hsi was meditating by a river when he saw an animal resembling a dragon climb from the water. It was like nothing he had seen before, and he was drawn to the lines on its scales. Having looked at these lines for a time, he felt inspired and decided that the creature had appeared to help him and others in their quest for knowledge. He therefore set about drawing a series of diagrams (using the lines on the animal's scales as a basis) which would be complete enough to contain all wisdom. Other stories suggest that Fu Hsi devised what became known as the trigrams after studying the pattern on a tortoise shell. Indeed, in ancient times tortoise shells were often used in divination.

The basis for I Ching

There is no need to understand Eastern philosophies to understand the Book of Changes. All that is necessary is to be able to comprehend the idea of polarities.

To Westerners, polarity may mean opposites, as in negative and positive. To understand I Ching it is necessary to abandon these ideas, and understand that seemingly opposing energies can be complementary. In the same way as night follows day without division, it is necessary to understand that nothing is fixed, nothing is split into past, present or future, and that everything is interlinked and constantly changing.

One of the main principles of I Ching is that energy comes in two forms – yang (active, masculine and powerful) and yin (passive, feminine and gentle). You may have already come across a symbol for this, which is also used by students of T'ai Chi.

I Ching holds that everything in the universe as we know it is generated from the yin–yang polarity. Yang relates to the sun and yin the moon. Hence we arrive at day and night, light and dark, male and female, positive and negative, and so on. Likewise, yang controls heaven and yin controls earth. Even the seasons relate to the theory, summertime having more yang and wintertime more yin.

In I Ching, yang, positive, active and masculine is represented by a straight line.

Yin on the other hand, being passive and feminine is represented by a line of the same length but broken.

From this concept, we move on to the four primary symbols, each represented by two lines.

Greater yang is shown thus:

Greater yin is shown thus:

Lesser yang is shown thus:

Lesser yin is shown thus

To these symbols were added another line, either yang or yin, to create what are known as the eight trigrams, which have names, directions, family links, complementary body areas, elements, seasons and elemental features.

What can I Ching tell us?

I Ching can help answer questions. In ancient times it was used merely to provide a Yes/No answer. Tradition suggests that tortoise shells were used. However, the developed version of I Ching that we now use can provide detailed information and advice, as well as self-knowledge.

What I Ching cannot do is give hard and fast rules on what must or must not be done in a situation. Its advice is given freely, but acknowledges the seeker's freedom of choice to accept or reject what is offered. It suggests options and gives advice both on understanding a situation and altering it, but it leaves the person concerned to make their own decision. Having a situation clarified can often help in itself. I Ching can be witty, but it is also very wise and can be exceptionally accurate if used properly and with firm intent.

It is pointless to pose a question which demands a Yes/No answer, such as 'Shall I move or not?' In this case it would be better to ask, 'Will a move be beneficial?'

I Ching in the modern age

I Ching is as relevant today as it ever was. Its teachings are universal and timeless. Moreover, it is easy to use, accurate and precise. It can also be used by an individual, without the need for a consultation with an expert. It is the true do-it-yourself manual.

I Ching requires no psychic talent, no divination and no research. You don't need dates, numbers, ages or planetary positions. You don't have to remember a lot of symbols, and you don't need to understand a foreign language or even any Eastern terminology. All you need is a question and a genuine need for an answer – and of course the ability to draw a series of straight lines!

At the end of our studies, it is hoped that you will look on I Ching as a true and wise friend.

THE FOUNDATIONS

OF I CHING

A lthough no one knows the exact age of the Book of Changes, it is certainly one of the oldest and most spiritual books we have. That it has survived when other books of its time have not is an indication of its lasting value. This chapter looks at the basis of I Ching.

Westerners sometimes find the poetry of the Book of Changes complicated and obscure. It can indeed prove difficult to understand, probably because it seems to relate more to Mandarin lords than to our modern age. We will, however, discuss not only the translations but the modern counterpart.

I Ching basically concerns what Jung called 'synchronicity' – a way of looking at things which connects one to another in unexpected ways. For example you might be thinking of someone, and then, apparently out of the blue, they turn up on your doorstep. Conversely, you might want the answer to a question and then find it, apparently by chance, in a magazine article you happen to be reading.

I Ching requires a certain amount of study before it is fully understood; even Confucius felt that the many years he spent were inadequate. The aim here is to help the beginner to get a footing on the ladder of understanding. There will still be many rungs to climb.

The original format of I Ching was eight trigrams. The Book of Changes tells of the Great Primal Beginning, which brought about two primary forces (yin and yang), and two primary trigrams. These generated four images, which in turn generated the eight trigrams on which I Ching is based. These trigrams are shown here surrounding the yin and yang symbols, believed to represent the whole of the universe. This drawing is based on the Pak Kua charm, which is often used by students of Feng Shui as a protective measure. We will briefly discuss Feng Shui in Chapter 2.

LEGEND OR FACT?

It is said that the 64 hexagrams now used were formulated by King Wen, a feudal lord who was one of the founders of the Chou dynasty and a student of Tao (pronounced *Dow*). Tao or 'the way' concerns the hidden 'Principle of the Universe' and focuses on harmony between mankind and the environment. Students of Taoism feel more inclined to seek answers to their questions in meditation than by seeking direct help. In modern parlance, Tao could be said to be a person's natural direction in life.

I Ching aims to show ways around blockages in that natural direction or way. Taoism teaches that there are two main energy sources, yin and yang, feminine and masculine, and all the wisdom of I Ching comes from the interaction of these two forces.

In 1143 BC, King Wen was imprisoned by the Emperor and sentenced to death. Whilst in prison he paired up the trigrams already in existence to form six-line figures – hexagrams – which he arranged either in circular or square pattern. He named these hexagrams and wrote a commentary called the T'uan which explained each hexagram and gave advice. Sometimes this is called the Judgement. King Wen's son, the Duke of Chou, then added a

commentary on the individual lines within the hexagrams and on the symbolism involved. Sometimes this is called the Image, but also Hsiang Chuan. The addition of 384 commentaries became a vital part of the finished product. What came about from all this work is the Book of Changes as we now know it, comprising combinations of all the paired trigrams and the Judgements upon them.

Several centuries later, Confucius and his students edited the book and added the further commentary and text known as the Ten Wings. According to this commentary, 'Change has an absolute limit: This produces two modes: The two modes produce four forms, the four forms produce eight trigrams; The eight trigrams determine fortune and misfortune.' This statement summarises the whole basis for I Ching. The paragraphs of commentary on the judgements of King Wen are often called T'uan Chuan.

In 213 BC, the Emperor Ch'in Shih Huang Ti ordered many books to be burned, including the Confucian commentaries on I Ching. Fortunately some copies survived. It is worth remembering that the original production of I Ching would not have been in book form as we now understand this. Most probably it would have been written on strips of wood or bamboo.

The Book of Changes continued to be held in high esteem after the time of Confucius, and during the time of the Han dynasty (202 BC–AD 220) the diagrams were given religious principles. In 136 BC imperial authorities sponsored a special study of the work. By AD 175, five Confucian books, including I Ching, were engraved in stone so that they would never be lost to mankind. During the Sung dynasty (960–1279) further revisions were made and a commentary by the philosopher Chu Hsi was added. By 1715, one edition of the book included commentaries from 218 different scholars, dating back to the second century BC.

Modern I Ching

The introduction of I Ching to the West began in the early 1800s in France, but it became more widely known through the work of a

German Christian missionary called Richard Wilhelm, who came across it whilst in China. It is said that a group of Taoists asked if they might teach him something about Taoism in exchange for his teaching them something of Christianity. He became so interested in what he learned that he began work on German translations of several Taoist texts, including the Book of Changes. His resulting book is called The Secret of the Golden Flower. The most influential work on I Ching was done by Richard Wilhelm, who translated the work, based on the K'ang Hsi edition published in 1715, into German, from whence it has frequently been translated into English. This work was the impetus behind his writing The Secret of the Golden Flower. A translation of I Ching had appeared in English in 1899, published by James Legge in Oxford, but had not received as much notice, probably because of the fact that Legge was a sinologist and the text was written for other sinologists.

In more recent times Carl Jung, the Swiss analytical psychologist, became interested in I Ching, originally seeking to prove it useless, but then discovering it to be a means of obtaining self-knowledge. It is said that Jung spent most of one summer sitting under a pear tree casting hexagrams and was so impressed with the results that he decided to use I Ching to help his patients.

I Ching doesn't think in terms of past, present and future; it thinks in terms of possibilities. It is necessary to understand this at the outset. Taoism believes that nothing is fixed or permanent, and that everything changes. This principle is essential to understanding I Ching.

Many modern Chinese leaders have used I Ching, including Mao Zedong and Chiang Kai-Shek. The popularity of I Ching and the ease with which it relates to computer technology has led to it being more widely used than ever, with battery-powered, hand-held I Ching computers now available in some parts of the world.

Students of astrology might be interested to know that I Ching was antedated by the T'ai Hsuan Ching, and that this in turn owed its existence to the Lunar Mansions of Chinese astrology. As we will shortly discuss, the 64 hexagrams of I Ching are each made up of two trigrams. These trigrams have archetypal values that relate to solar astrology. However, this subject is perhaps better left to later study. It is, however, important to realise that I Ching and astrology do have certain parallels.

CONSULTING I CHING

All of us at some time or another need help in finding our true direction. To some people, consulting a professional counsellor provides the answer, while others prefer to consult the Tarot, the Runes or some other divinatory source. For those who seek not only guidance but also a spiritual wisdom, I Ching is the ideal method. In addition, it is not necessary to consult with another person for this guidance. All you need is the Book of Changes itself, and either three coins or a set of sticks, as we shall shortly discuss.

I Ching concerns change and regeneration. Change itself becomes the focus of attention rather than the question or questioner, known as 'the Superior Man'. Change can be both negative and positive, and it is worth noting that the 'I' of I Ching is normally translated as 'change'. The object is to learn to use change to your advantage, to work with it rather than opposing it, and thus become creative, letting go of the past and any outmoded conditioning. Nothing is fixed. If you alter the present, the future will also be altered. I Ching offers ways of altering the present and the future.

I Ching brings to the surface three sorts of change – non-change, cyclic change and sequent change, and relates to significant coincidences. Non-change does not mean lack of movement, but change which remains static or unchangeable. Cyclic change works in the same way as the seasons, whilst sequent change is progressive, relating to generations, and is produced by cause and effect.

I Ching does not say what is going to happen. It relates to the paths of action open to us, leaving us to meditate on our final choice. The person asking the question always remains apart from I Ching itself. The hexagrams are consulted, and the text read, and the questioner then has to look within to find his or her way.

Asking questions

How we formulate the question is crucial. Remember to ask specifics, not just vague questions. I Ching will answer anything put to it properly, giving possible courses of action and directions from which to choose by bringing into play our own personal intuition on the matter in hand. We are not given set parameters, but a freedom of choice and the responsibility for making the final decision for ourselves.

As I Ching is old and wise, it should be treated as an old and wise counsellor. Thinking of it in this way, try imagining how you would address such a sage. You wouldn't waste their time, but would treat them with respect and value the guidance given.

Be respectful and serious of intent when consulting I Ching. Think hard about the situation in which you find yourself, adopting a reflective state of mind before formulating a question so that the answer can be clear. Having consulted I Ching, interpret the answers given in terms of the question asked and make your own decision from there.

Consider writing the question down, altering the wording until you feel it is perfect, and then starting the consultation process. The question must have a single answer, rather than a series of possibilities. Some people speak the question out loud, altering it to suit until they are satisfied. The way you formulate your question is up to you. However, once you have arrived at the wording, you can expect the answer to be equally precise and clear.

Methods of consultation

There is more than one way of consulting I Ching. One of the traditional methods uses grains of rice. Another employs yarrow sticks, allegedly because yarrow grows on the grave of Confucius. Using yarrow sticks is definitely more complex and takes time. If you feel it better to use traditional methods, or methods which allow more time for reflection to take place, use yarrow sticks.

Another method adopted by the Chinese is the use of six marked wands. These wands are painted black with a white bar across one side. They are thrown onto the ground, picked up, beginning with the rod nearest the caster and read. Those showing the white bar are yin; those that do not are yang. A problem then arises in that we have no 'moving lines', about which more later, and the Duke of Chou's commentary does not come into play. The main methods used in the West, however, remain either yarrow sticks or coins. These are described in detail below.

Coins

If you decide to try the coin system, you will find the whole process much easier and quicker than using yarrow sticks, which can take between half an hour and an hour. Using coins takes a minute or so at the outside.

It is not essential to use Chinese coins. However, if you have access to a shop which sells these, use them by all means. Many people, myself included, use old Chinese cash coins. These are round coins with square central holes. They were used once as currency but are now used mainly for I Ching. If using these coins, it is necessary to understand which is 'heads' and which is 'tails'. The side of the coin with four characters is the yang side (shown as a solid line) with a value of 3, whilst the other side which normally has nothing inscribed on it has a value of 2, and represents yin (a broken line.) If you are using other coins, use coppers if possible. The 'head' side of the coin is normally given the yang character, whilst the 'tail' side of the coin is given the yin line.

Shake three coins and throw them down when it feels right to you to do so. There is no time limit here, and again you might like to think about the question and its form while doing this. When you have thrown the coins down, count their value, remembering which side represents 2 and which 3. Add these together. The value of each throw will be six, seven, eight or nine. Write down the line for each throw, starting at the bottom and working up. Write down the numbers first if that helps. The lines for each value are shown below. The significance of 'moving' lines (old yin or old yang) is discussed in Chapter 2.

A short cut might be to look to see whether the majority of coins fall with heads upwards. These would represent a yang line, whilst if they fell with the majority downwards, you would have a yin line. Take care to remember the 'moving' lines in this shortcut! If all the coins fall the same way up, the situation is considered to be 'moving' or unbalanced, signifying imminent change. Three 2s are known as 'moving yin', as shown above, and three 3s are 'moving yang', again as shown above. All moving lines, as we will see in the next chapter, become their opposites given time.

YARROW STICKS

If you decide to use yarrow sticks, you need a bundle of 50 sticks – traditionally bamboo or wood, although I have seen other things used, such as matchsticks (not recommended). If you wanted to use the traditional yarrow, you would need to use the stalks of the plant *Achillea millefolium*. The sticks must be the same length.

Traditionally, you should begin by facing south, with the oracle in front of you, a small incense tray and the container for the yarrow sticks to the side. The Chinese burn incense in their tray, take the yarrow sticks in the right hand, and pass them through the incense smoke, in a clockwise motion, keeping the sticks horizontal. This is done to help formulate the question. This done, remove one stick from the bundle and put it aside. Traditionally this is done with the right hand. This stick will not be used. You are now left with 49, which students of numerology will know relates to the number 7 (7×7) which has special powers.

The 49 sticks are divided randomly into two piles. A stick from the right-hand pile is placed between the ring finger and little finger of the left hand. The left-hand pile is then counted through in fours, and the remainder, which will be four or less, is then inserted between the ring finger and middle finger of the left hand. This process is repeated for the right pile, and the remaining stalks are inserted between the middle and index fingers of the left hand. You now find yourself with a total of either five or nine stalks between the fingers of your left hand. Lay these stalks aside, mix the two remaining piles together, and repeat the process all over again twice. The second and third times, you will find the stalks in your hand will number either four or eight.

The first line of the hexagram is the lowest line, and your subsequent lines will go on top. The first line is determined by the number of sticks you have in each of your three piles. A pile with a total of eight or nine sticks is given a value of 2. A pile with a total of four or five sticks has a value of 3. It is necessary to add together the value of the three piles. Three 2s indicates what is known as a 'moving' yin line, shown with a cross: ————×———— . These 'moving' lines signify a changing situation. They are discussed in more detail in Chapter 2. If you have two 2s and a three, a yang line or ———————— is indicated. One two and two 3s produces a yin line or ——— ——— and three 3s a moving yang line, shown with a circle: ————⊙———— .

To find the remaining five lines to go on top of this base line and complete the hexagram it is necessary to repeat the whole procedure five times. As you can see, all this takes a lot of time.

You may wonder at this point why one stick is taken away at the start. If we are to use 49 sticks, why start with 50? The reasons behind this are numerous, but one way of thinking is that 50 is the whole, and you are taking away from the whole. The stick you don't use becomes the something which gives rise to all things.

Another way of looking at I Ching is well illustrated by the Taoist philosopher Lao Tsu. Commenting on I Ching he said: 'We put thirty spokes together and call it a wheel. It is, however, on the spaces where there is nothing that the utility of the wheel depends.'

Drawing the hexagram

The hexagram is composed of six lines which are either broken or unbroken. They represent yin and yang, masculine and feminine, light and dark. We have arrived at the stage of drawing the hexagram from bottom to top by the methods discussed above. The hexagrams are 64 combinations of lines, each with a specific name.

Let us now assume that we have the hexagram drawn, and that, for the sake of ease, there are no moving lines. We could end up with something like this:

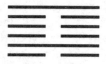

Hexagram 4

We would now merely seek to find that hexagram amongst the others, using the table on page 24. Firstly, we would read the description of the hexagram – its title. Let's say we are looking at hexagram 4, shown above, which is Innocence, or Youthful Inexperience, as we shall shortly see. It also has the Chinese name Meng. Innocence, again as we shall see, is made up of the trigram 'Water/Deep' or K'an, followed by Ken or 'Mountain'. We read the description. We then move on to the overall judgement and read that, before moving on to the image.

Most interpretations go on to break this down line by line. Some students of I Ching suggest that this is unnecessary, feeling it tends to analyse too much, rather than 'going with the flow', which is the main focus of Tao. I make no judgements one way or the other, but it is worth remembering that the Duke of Chou looked at individual lines and their meanings. I will give these line meanings and you can make up your own mind as to whether or not to use them. I will also give a modern interpretation of the whole, for those who find the poetry and allegory of the original translation difficult to understand or who seek a quick answer.

It is also then possible to look for the opposite hexagram as well as another hexagram which complements the original. All this, however, can complicate matters, and is perhaps best left to professional I Ching readers or to further study at a future date.

It is now necessary, before finishing this section, to look at the eight trigrams which make up the hexagrams. It is very important to understand these, as we will be giving trigram breakdowns when discussing each hexagram. They are a vital element of each hexagram meaning.

As we know, these have names in both English and Chinese. We will discuss both. Each trigram also has other connections, and these will be listed as we progress. It should be noted that the direction link is that suggested by King Wen, not Fu Hsi.

The eight trigrams

Ch'ien

K'un

Chen

Sun

K'an

Li

Ken

Tui

The eight trigrams are produced by four forms of yin and yang, and are known as major or minor. These are as follows:

> Major yang trigrams: Heaven and Marsh
> Minor yin trigrams: Thunder and Fire
> Major yin trigrams: Earth and Mountain
> Minor yang trigrams: Water and Wind

We will now look at each trigram in more detail.

Ch'ien

English name: Heaven/Sky
Keyword: Creative
Family member: Father
Animal link: Horse
Body link: Head
Element: Metal
Colour: Purple
Season: Early winter
Direction: North-west
Polarity: Yang

Ch'ien is creative originality in all things. It relates to fortunate change to achieve balance and to inspiration, aggressiveness, completeness, power and coldness. Design and training are suggested, as also is management. Ch'ien's three unbroken lines are said to represent strength, vitality and good fortune.

K'un

English name: Earth
Keyword: Receptive
Family member: Mother
Animal link: Cow
Body link: Solar plexus
Element: Soil
Colour: Black
Season: Early autumn
Direction: South-west
Polarity: Yin

K'un relates to the feminine, and to submission, charity, evenness, protectiveness and faithfulness. It suggests health matters, welfare, nourishment and things relating to children. It is the direct opposite of Ch'ien.

Chen

English name: Thunder
Keyword: Arousing
Family member: Eldest son
Animal link: Dragon
Body link: Foot
Element: Grass
Colour: Orange
Season: Spring
Direction: East
Polarity: Yang

Chen relates to movement, experimentation and development, impulsiveness and speed. It suggests transport, roads and distribution.

Sun

English name: Wind/Wood
Keyword: Gentleness
Family member: Eldest daughter
Animal link: Cat
Body link: Thighs
Element: Air
Colour: White
Season: Early summer
Direction: South-east
Polarity: Yin

Sun represents growth of vegetation, fragmentation, and pliability. It also concerns trade, routine and factory operations.

K'an

English name: Water/Deep/Moon
Keyword: Abyss
Family member: Middle son
Animal link: Pig
Body link: Ear
Element: Wood

Colour: Red
Season: Winter
Direction: North
Polarity: Yang

K'an represents danger. Symbolic of thought and concentration, this trigram suggests work and melancholy. It also concerns garages and machinery.

Li

English name: Fire/Sun
Keyword: Separation
Family member: Middle daughter
Animal link: Bird
Body link: Eye
Element: Fire
Colour: Yellow
Season: Summer
Direction: South
Polarity: Yin

Li represents enlightenment, clarity, adherence, firmness and beauty. It connects with communication, as well as with the kitchen, ovens, furnaces and any form of heating.

Ken

English name: Mountain
Keyword: Blockage
Family member: Youngest son
Animal link: Dog
Body link: Hand
Element: Stone
Colour: Green
Season: Early spring
Direction: North-east
Polarity: Yang

Ken represents carefulness, inevitability and modesty. It is perfection and stillness. It connects with security, barriers and any form of doorway or entrance.

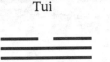

Tui	English name: Marsh/Mist/Lake
	Keyword: Happiness
	Family member: Youngest daughter
	Animal link: Sheep
	Body link: Mouth
	Element: Flesh
	Colour: Blue
	Season: Autumn
	Direction: West
	Polarity: Yin

Tui represents pleasure, sensuality and magic, through progress and achievement. It connects with recreation, entertainment and enjoyment.

We have now covered the main basic elements of I Ching, and must further learn about moving lines and the sovereign hexagrams. These and other concerns, appear in the next chapter.

PRACTICE

Before we look at the meaning of moving lines in Chapter 2, let's take a few practice throws using what we have already learned and see whether we feel comfortable with drawing the hexagrams. Remember to draw the hexagrams from bottom to top.

Let's just draw one, and use the coin system, because it's quicker. Let's say we throw as follows:

1st throw – Two 2s and one 3
2nd throw – Two 2s and one 3
3rd throw – One 2 and two 3s
4th throw – Three 3s
5th throw – Two 2s and one 3
6th throw – Three 2s

How would you draw this hexagram? If you are in doubt, do your best and then try again after reading Chapter 2, as (hint) there are some moving lines there!

I CHING IN PRACTICE AND IN CONTEXT

We have briefly mentioned moving lines in our last chapter, and now we must look at these in more detail. We must think in terms of 'old yang' and 'old yin', and 'young yang' and 'young yin'. The principle behind the moving lines is that the universe is in constant flux.

The chapter also looks at sovereign hexagrams, Taoism and Feng Shui, or Chinese geomancy.

MOVING LINES

Moving lines are lines which are not fixed. Young yang and young yin are the lines in their 'normal' form, i.e. not changing. Old yang and old yin, however, are not, and are shown differently.

According to Confucius, when a power reaches its culmination, it becomes 'old'. It then changes to its opposite. An old yang line, shown ———⊖——— is in the process of moving from yang to yin and will become ——— ——— and likewise with old yin, shown ———✕——— will become ———————. As we know, change is a fundamental part of I Ching. Yin and yang do not remain static but are always interrelating.

When you cast your coins or throw your yarrow sticks, you are more or less certain to get a moving line, which is made by the 6 or 9. The 6 line is old yin ———✕———, and the 9 line is old yang ———⊖———. When this appears, it is necessary to draw a further hexagram, thus:

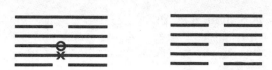

It is necessary to read both hexagrams, taking into account the different meanings of the moving lines when looking at the individual line meanings. Of course, if the hexagram has no moving lines, it is simple, as the situation is either unmoving or ending. Moving lines indicate areas of change and of particular note. Moving lines indicate that the situation is unbalanced, being too positive or too negative, and thus liable to change also.

PRACTICE

Let's do a little practice on that first. Using coins (the quicker method), do a few practice throws, and see how many times you get either 6 or 9 in your calculations. That will, as we now know, indicate a moving line. Maybe you want to look back to the hexagram we discussed at the end of Chapter 1 where the throws were given for you, and see how you did, and whether you were right. Your hexagram should look like this:

Practise drawing the moving lines, and remember we are reading the lines from bottom to top, the bottom line being line 1 and so on upwards. Also practise altering the hexagram to show how the moving lines have changed the hexagram. Remember, when we have moving lines, we have to think in terms of two hexagrams being drawn.

You may have wondered why hexagrams are drawn from the bottom upwards. One explanation for this bottom to top drawing which corresponds to the Chinese way of writing characters is that it is in accord with nature, where it is seen that things grow from the bottom (soil) upwards.

Let's recap using the following illustration as an explanation:

Two 2s and one 3 = Yang
Two 3s and one 2 = Yin
Three 3s = Moving yang
Three 2s = Moving yin

Remember ——⊙—— becomes —— —— , and
——✗—— becomes ————

SOVEREIGN HEXAGRAMS

It is said that I Ching was used by the ancient Chinese as an addition to their lunar calendar. Twelve hexagrams were allotted to the 12 months, and called Sovereign. It is said that if one of these hexagrams appeared in a reading, an indication was being given of the likely timing of forthcoming events.

These hexagrams are known as T'ai, Ta Chuang, Kuai, Ch'ien, Kou, Tun, P'i, Kuan, Po, K'un, Fu and Lin respectively, and the table below will adequately explain the time spans and the names of the fortnight periods to which they relate.

HEXAGRAM	NAMES OF FORTNIGHTS	COMMENCING
T'ai	Beginning of Spring	5 February
	The Rains	20 February
Ta Chuang	Awakening of Creatures	7 March
	Spring Equinox	22 March

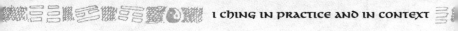

Kuai

Clear and Bright	6 April
Grain Rain	21 April

Ch'ien

Beginning of Summer	6 May
Lesser Fullness	22 May

Kou

Grain in Ear	7 June
Summer Solstice	22 June

Tun

Lesser Heat	8 July
Greater Heat	24 July

P'i

Beginning of Autumn	8 August
End of Heat	24 August

Kuan

White Dews	8 September
Autumn Equinox	24 September

Po

Cold Dews	9 October
Descent of Hoar Frost	24 October

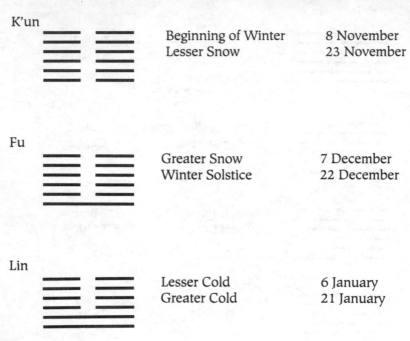

K'un

Beginning of Winter	8 November
Lesser Snow	23 November

Fu

Greater Snow	7 December
Winter Solstice	22 December

Lin

Lesser Cold	6 January
Greater Cold	21 January

PRACTICE

Consider the following example:

1st throw – Two 2s and one 3
2nd throw – Two 2s and one 3
3rd throw – Two 2s and one 3
4th throw – Two 3s and one 2
5th throw – Two 3s and one 2
6th throw – Two 3s and one 2

Firstly, think how this hexagram is drawn. Which line goes at the bottom? When you have drawn this hexagram, you should find

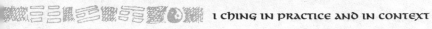

that you end up with one of the sovereign hexagrams. Which one? If you were asked to find the time span here, what would you say? What are the first three lines, yin or yang, and what about the second set of three lines?

Need an answer? The answer is that you would end up with the hexagram called T'ai, and the time span would be 5 February or 20 February commencement. The first three lines are yang, and the second three lines are yin. These two trigrams, then, are major yang followed by major yin. Did you remember to draw the hexagram from the bottom up? Did you get the answer yourself, or did you wait until I gave it? Remember, practice makes perfect!

Before we finish this section, let's look at the two trigrams that make up the above hexagram. Remember, each hexagram is made up of two trigrams. The first trigram we have is three yang lines. If you remember, these represent Heaven and are given the name Ch'ien. The second trigram we have is three yin lines. You will recall that these represent Earth and are given the name K'un. In this one hexagram, then, which is one of the sovereign hexagrams, we have the two symbols of heaven and earth in harmony, one with the other, in the same way as feminine (mother) and masculine (father) are in harmony.

Remember the hexagrams are combinations of the eight trigrams. It is important to think of the whole hexagram, its trigrams and its individual lines.

Looking back before moving forward

We are nearly at the point where we can start to look at each hexagram individually. However, before we progress to that point, it is necessary to backtrack a little to look at the I Ching and its relationship to Tao, considered by the Chinese to be the Absolute Truth.

As we know, Tao is 'the way'. It is said that I Ching inspired the mystic Lao-tzu, who it is said lived to more than 200 years of age, to write Tao Teh Ching, or 'The Classic of the Way of its Virtue', which is the central text of Taoism. Taoism is the only indigenous religion of China. It promotes 'going with the flow' or Wu-Wei, softness, kindness and humility, rather than aggression and toughness. This is the relationship between yin and yang. It further teaches that one of the main ways towards understanding is meditation and correct breathing, or as Lao-tzu suggested 'breathing permanently like the infant' with light breathing to such an extent that it appears to outward inspection as though the person concerned is hardly breathing at all.

As we know, the method of consulting the I Ching using yarrow stalks focuses very much on a meditative state, rather more so than using the coins. It is worthwhile remembering that the I Ching represents an entire philosophy and way of life. It symbolises a cyclical universe, and a path which follows fixed laws, with only meaningful coincidences. It encourages one to look within, and does not give 'Yes, but'/'No, but' answers. It shows that we can all be at one with the environment and with nature.

It is worth noting at this point that traditionally 'Yes, but'/'No, but' answers used to be a part of I Ching. The solid yang line or ———— was said to indicate a 'Yes' answer, whilst the broken yin line or —— —— signified a 'No' answer. By adding a further line thus —— —— it is said you could come up with a 'Yes, but...' answer, or a 'No, but' answer when —— —— was drawn. Obviously when forming trigrams and hexagrams, these indications prove useless.

I Ching is a form which requires us to look within ourselves for the answer given various choices or suggestions. It reflects the moment in time at which the hexagram is drawn and shows a probable outcome with various alternatives. Most students of I Ching would feel that a 'Yes, but'/'No, but' answer was cheating them of an opportunity for spiritual development.

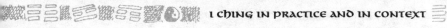

The Feng Shui connection

We have briefly mentioned Feng Shui and the protection charm used which incorporates I Ching, and before we finish this section, we will look a little more at this.

Feng Shui is known in the Western world largely by the term 'Geomancy'. Feng Shui concerns the positioning of buildings, etc., to receive the best vibrations from the earth, and its literal translation is 'wind and water'.

As with I Ching, its origins link with Taoism, but also with nature patterns, astrology and numerology. It is largely practised in the East, and, like I Ching, is made up of yin and yang elements. In Feng Shui the lines are made up of one or two crosses, rather than the unbroken and broken lines used in I Ching.

Those who have studied both I Ching and Feng Shui in detail suggest that there are various parallels between the 64 hexagrams and the 16 symbols of Feng Shui/geomancy. There are obvious differences, one of the main being that the geomantic figures used in the Western version of Feng Shui (which comprise four lines rather than six) are drawn from top to bottom. However, those who have studied geomancy suggest that linking the two forms produces a depth each form independently lacks.

Feng Shui is a very involved subject, but it is important for the beginner to realise the links here, so that further study of I Ching can take them into account. If you would like to find out more about Feng Shui, you might like to consult another book in this series – *Feng Shui For Beginners*, by Richard Craze, Headway, 1994. It shows how to use Feng Shui in your everyday life, as well as explaining the history and theory of this ancient Chinese philosophy.

In the next chapter, we will start to look in detail at the hexagrams. It is necessary to familiarise yourself with the chart shown on the following page, which gives all hexagrams and their numbers. Their names will be given as we discuss each hexagram.

Key to the hexagrams

Upper Trigrams / Lower Trigrams	☰	☱	☲	☳	☴	☵	☶	☷
☰	1	43	34	14	11	26	5	9
☱	10	58	54	38	19	41	60	61
☲	25	17	51	21	24	27	3	42
☳	13	49	55	30	36	22	63	37
☴	12	45	16	35	2	23	8	20
☵	33	31	62	56	15	52	39	53
☶	6	47	40	64	7	4	29	59
☷	44	28	32	50	46	18	48	57

3 the hexagrams

*T*his chapter covers the 64 individual hexagrams of the I Ching. Note that although they are all represented by different Chinese characters, when transliterated into English several of them are repeated: for example, (1) Ch'ien The Creative and (15) Ch'ien Humility. This is purely because of the limitations of transliteration. Many users prefer to use the English names in order to avoid confusion.

The translation used is that of Richard Wilhelm, rendered into English from Wilhelm's German by Cary F. Baynes. However, the work of James Legge is also taken into account. Each hexagram is dealt with in four sections: interpretation, judgement, image and line meanings. The interpretation covers basic understanding, plus elements of the commentary section of the original Book of Changes.

Drawing the Hexagrams

The lines are given working from the first line, which goes at the bottom, upwards. As you will know, the throwing of three heads or three tails (6 or 9) brings about moving lines. Lines which are not subject to moving are brought about by throwing a combination of heads and tails (7 or 8). Please bear this in mind and remember that with moving lines it is necessary to construct the new hexagram and look at the changes.

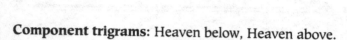

(1) Ch'ien – The Creative

Component trigrams: Heaven below, Heaven above.

Modern meaning: Success is assured, as strength, power and persistence are yours. Continue with your plans, but don't overreach yourself.

Interpretation

This hexagram is total yang, there being no yin elements within it. It represents heaven, god and the power of the creative. It is the universe, the holy man and true spirit. Ch'ien conforms and changes, transforms and moves. It is part of evolution.

Judgement

> Sublime success through perseverance
> As creative power permeates all heaven:
> By clouds and rain all beings attain form,
> So the great man sees, with great clarity, causes and effects.
> By persevering does he complete things in their due time.
> Each end is a new beginning.

Things will happen when they are meant; an ending is merely a means to a new start. Things move in cycles. It is necessary to have patience.

Image

> As heaven moves with unceasing power,
> So the wise man becomes strong and untiring.

Evolution continues no matter what. The wise person learns to develop and move forward. Be strong and work hard, and with the help of 'the heavens' you will succeed.

Line meanings

Line 1

> Creative power that is still hidden
> When the time is not ripe, do not act.

James Legge refers to the creative power throughout as 'the dragon'. This corresponds with the Duke of Chou's work, where the dragon represented the 'superior man'. Wait for a better time before acting, and learn the power of patience. You will instinctively know when the time has come to act. You must not force anything.

Line 2

> Creative power that stirs in the field.

Things start to move and develop. You meet, or should actively seek to meet, someone who is able to help you through their influence. Any partnership or joining together would be profitable.

Line 3

> Creative power that becomes known
> But dangers lurk in the rise to fame.

Power brings with it great responsibilities. Use this wisely and well. Try to stay above gossip and guard against over-ambition. Think about what you are doing. You may feel anxious, but don't create problems through this anxiety.

Line 4

> To weigh and waver. Where is one's way?

Weigh up the pros and cons of the situation and make sure there are no mistakes. It is up to you to move forward or stay put. Make the choice yourself.

Line 5

> Creative power accords with heaven.

Like the wise man, work with the heavens, move forward and become influential. Legge suggests that when flying dragons are in the heavens, the time is right to try to meet with other influential people, if possible. You will be popular now, and others will seek you out.

Line 6

> Creative power that goes too far:
> Arrogance will bring cause to repent.

Sometimes those who rise in power and station become divorced from the man in the street. It is necessary to remain in touch with the people and with reality. Don't exceed your own limitations. This would lead to failure.

Moving lines – if you have drawn a hexagram with all the yang lines as moving lines, this shows a balance between mind, body and spirit, and things are well with you. It is a lucky time.

(2) K'un – The Receptive

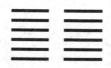

Other keywords: Resting in Firmness.

Component trigrams: Earth below, Earth above.

Modern meaning: The future looks good, but may lie in the hands

of others. Be quiet, responsive and receptive. Try not to force the issue. Things will happen in their own time.

Interpretation

This hexagram is the power of yin, there being no yang elements within it. It represents the person who seeks to serve, who is passive and receptive, but also action, which is direct and inspired. This hexagram allows a meditation for inspiration. It also suggests solitude and contact with the inner self, leading to a rebirth.

Judgement

> The receptive is strong, yet devoted.
> If one tries to lead, one loses oneself.

This suggests that it may be better to find the creative (masculine) to lead the receptive (feminine). It is necessary both to be strong and also seek to serve.

Image

> As is the earth's nature: strong, devoted,
> Thus does a wise man carry the outer world.

The earth supports, sustains and protects, and you should live in harmony with this strength, as it is your partner. Likewise, you should live in harmony with others, as they will also support you.

Line meanings

Line 1

> When hoarfrost is underfoot
> Solid ice is not far off. Be vigilant.

Solid ice is yin. If you keep going, you will find a solid footing. Watch for things that are not solid and firm.

LINE 2

> Be like nature: true, calm and great;
> Without design, yet furthering all.

Yin is considered to be honest, straight, dutiful and consistent. Be likewise. Don't be overcome by doubt, as it will pass.

LINE 3

> Seek not works, but bring to completion
> Thus can one remain persevering.

Act when the time is right, not before. Legge's translation also refers to government work, and therefore anything involving public life should be viewed with restraint, with others receiving the accolades rather than yourself. You will learn by watching others, and have no need to seek credit for yourself.

LINE 4

> When in danger, strictest reticence.

Be careful to avoid harm. Be reserved and cautious. By remaining quiet and in solitude, you will neither come to nor receive harm. Legge's translation refers to 'a sack tied up'. Keeping 'the sack' tied up would be safer than opening it. Watch what you say.

LINE 5

> Genuineness and utmost discretion.
> Gracefulness comes from within.

Be reserved. If you are looking for elevation in status, this will come from adopting a quiet approach. Legge's translation refers to 'a yellow garment' which was a sign of culture and high esteem.

LINE 6

> If one tries to rule, one is overthrown.

If you remain passive, steadfast and true, you will succeed. Be creative. If you become self-opinionated or resist the changes around you, you will fail; likewise will you fail if you occupy a position to which you are not entitled.

Moving lines – if you have drawn a hexagram with all lines moving, this indicates that, whilst you might be subject to mood or emotional swings, you are well balanced and move in harmony with the universe.

(3) Chun – Initial Difficulty

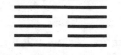

Other keywords: Growing pains/resolving chaos/germination.

Component trigrams: Thunder below, Water above.

Modern meaning: There are opportunities which could spell danger. Help may be needed. Let others give that help. Tread slowly and carefully. It's early days yet.

Interpretation

A period of confusion, chaos, difficulty and danger. Thunder can itself be dangerous, as can water to those who cannot swim. Tension is high. A spiritual awakening is suggested, and a chance to grow and learn.

Judgement

> Chaos and darkness whilst heaven creates.
> In times of difficulty at the beginning,
> Persevere. Appoint helpers. Do not rest.
> In this way comes success.

New things often have teething troubles. These are expected, and you must not give up. Involve others. Once things are sorted out, they will run more smoothly.

Image

> By movement in the midst of danger,
> The wise man brings order out of confusion.

Patience will reap its rewards. Work diligently and quietly, and things will be well. Be flexible with your ideas and wishes.

Line meanings

Line 1

> Hesitation; hindrance. Appoint helpers
> Be steadfast. Rule by serving. Success.

Don't force the pace, even if everything appears to be at a standstill. Work with, rather than against, others. Think about your plans, but keep going towards your ultimate goal. Remain honest and true. Use your energies wisely and well.

Line 2

> If unexpected relief comes, be cautious.

Don't commit yourself to something without thinking long and hard about it. The pressure is on, so be careful. An offer of help is genuine, but you could end up involved with things which bring their own complications. Everything will come right in its own time, however long that may be. Take control of your life.

Line 3

> With no guide, a wise man will desist.

Legge refers to 'the deer without the guidance of the forester'. To proceed would be foolish and you would later regret your actions. Remain true to your own counsel.

LINE 4

> An opportunity to be seized.
> Let neither false pride,
> Nor false reserve deter one.

Take action. You may need some help, but it is there for you should you decide to take it. Things will work out well. Partnerships are favoured.

LINE 5

> When others interpose
> And distort one's intentions,
> One must be cautious, not forceful.

Watch what you do. Don't let others sway you from your way. Make sure you are understood, and your motives are clear. Others may not understand you right now. Don't rush ahead. Take time to listen to others. Make your way slowly until things look a little better.

LINE 6

> Despair. Bloody tears flow.

Either choose to sort out the problems around you or break away and start afresh. You can't allow the situation at present to continue for much longer. The decision is yours to make. Nothing lasts for ever, but sometimes things need a push to move forward.

(4) MENG — INNOCENCE

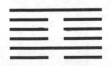

Other keywords: Immaturity/youthful ignorance and folly.

Component trigrams: Water below, Mountain above.

Modern meaning: You are lacking in experience or wisdom. Be enthusiastic and keep going, but learn at the same time. Take advice from those who are older or wiser.

Interpretation

Like the Fool card in the Tarot deck, this hexagram refers to youthful inexperience, rather than stupidity. New things can sometimes bring about danger, but if you listen to others, you will progress. Success will come about. Stick at it and learn. Ignorance is not just bliss; it can be dangerous. This hexagram refers to the beginner or newcomer, and can be taken to indicate 'beginner's luck'. It is important to retain the enthusiasm yet learn. There is also a spiritual innocence here. Meditation would be useful.

Judgement

> It is not I who seek the young fool:
> It is the young fool who seeks me.
> At first I inform him with clear answers;
> If he importunes, I tell him nothing.
> He must persevere to succeed.

The student must seek, and the teacher must wait to be sought. Both are dependent upon the other. The teacher cannot help without being asked, but the pupil must be respectful. If asked stupid questions, the teacher will not respond at all. Likewise, you must seek out the person or people who will give you answers, and prepare your questions. As we know, this is a major element of I Ching.

Image

> As a clear mountain spring flowing onward,
> So the wise man: thorough, clear and calm.

On our journey, we learn. As with Tarot, the fool goes on a journey of self-discovery, meeting people and situations along the way, to come round full circle, knowing more, but continuing with the journey. Likewise, you are told here to carry on along the way, achieving clarity of mind as you go. Calmness will help in the future, once learned.

Line meanings

Line 1

To make a fool develop, use discipline.
As discipline grows, the fetters should be removed.

The fetters here are fetters of the mind. Sometimes it is necessary to learn by mistakes or punishment. Provided such punishment is fairly dealt, there will be no problem. Learn self-discipline, but do not let it restrict you.

Line 2

To bear with fools kindly brings favour.

Legge's translation refers to the offspring taking charge of the family. Be firm, yet flexible. As you are still inexperienced, you will deal patiently with those who are foolish. This stands in your favour.

Line 3

Like a foolish girl, one loses oneself.

Don't let a stronger personality rule over you. They may be the epitome of everything you seek to be, but you should beware. Legge's translation refers to a young maiden meeting with a rich man. Don't take on a partnership with someone with whom you are incompatible.

Line 4

Entangled folly bring humiliation.

Make sure you stay in touch with reality. Fantasies belong in dreams and not in the real world. Anxieties about your inexperience may lead you to daydream. Watch this.

LINE 5

Childlike folly brings good fortune.

Simplicity is sometimes lucky. Humility is a good quality. Try to keep it. Arrogance should be avoided. Be optimistic.

LINE 6

Punish folly: but only to restore order.

Punishment is handed out as a learning opportunity. Order will then be restored. You have probably made some mistakes. Don't fret. Move on from there, and learn. Don't be angry with yourself, or with others who are ignorant and have many things to learn.

(5) Hsu – Waiting

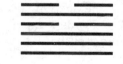

Other keywords: Nourishment/watering.

Component trigrams: Heaven below, Water above.

Modern meaning: It takes time for a crop to grow, and we must develop patience. Don't force the pace. Others will help when the time is right. Wait and be realistic. Don't worry.

Interpretation

Be sincere to succeed. There are streams to cross, but to do so now

could be dangerous. It will eventually be time to cross the stream, and you must stand firm.

Judgement

> If you are sincere: light and success.
> Be firm, strong, within; thus one avoids
> the danger of perplexity, bewilderment.
> Resolution equips one to meet one's fate.

Don't give up, but stand and wait. Have faith in yourself. Use the time to decide who and what you are, and what you want. Look at the reality of situations. See things clearly. This hexagram is all about self-control.

Image

> When clouds rise up to heaven
> The wise man eats and drinks.
> He is joyous and of good cheer.

Be happy with now. When the clouds rise up to the skies, the rain is not far behind, and a new growth will be nourished. Bide your time and enjoy.

Line meanings

Line 1

> When the danger is still far away
> Wait in a tranquil place. No blame.

Something is about to happen, but continue as before until that time arrives. You will know when that is, and be prepared to meet the challenges it brings. Keep calm and you won't go far wrong. Don't worry.

LINE 2

The danger appears. Gossip. Keep calm.

People may say things about you which upset you. Say nothing. It will all work out well in the end. Let them get on with it. Be prepared, however, for general upset. Don't blame other people if they seek to make you the scapegoat for a situation.

LINE 3

Entangled in danger. Be cautious.

Your anxieties have caused you to rush in too soon. Guard against further damage being done by remaining cautious, and wait.

LINE 4

Extreme danger. Get out of the pit.

You feel stuck. This was meant to happen. There is nothing you can do to change things. Keep calm. This is fate.

LINE 5

Waiting at meat and drink. Good cheer.

An oasis is offered in the desert. Use it wisely, but remember you must continue your journey. It is only a brief stop-over. Forget your troubles and take a break. Enjoy yourself for a time, and gather strength.

LINE 6

One falls into the pit. Stay alert.
Outside intervention brings rescue.

Stop analysing other people. Take any help offered, and be respectful, and you will receive good fortune. Even strangers can become friends with time! If your plans fail to turn out as hoped, the losses will be small.

(6) Sung — Contention

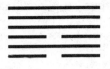

Other keywords: Conflict/dispute.

Component Trigrams: Heaven above, Water below.

Modern meaning: Learn to compromise. Don't act on impulse. Don't argue, and accept the criticism of others. Being aggressive is a waste of energy. Things will improve. Take advice.

Interpretation

Conflict is sometimes inevitable, and this hexagram is all about conflict. Learn to be less aggressive. Seek out those who are wise. Don't take on anything too large.

Judgement

> You are sincere but are obstructed,
> A cautious halt halfway brings favour.
> Going through to the end brings disfavour.
> Take advice. Seek a just arbiter.
> Great undertakings are not favoured.

You are alienating yourself from everyone around by continually saying you are right. Meet people halfway. You aren't always right, even if you are sure you must be. Listen to a third party. They may see things in a different light. Don't start any new contracts now. The timing is wrong.

Image

Heaven and water go their opposite ways.
A wise man considers his plans' beginnings.

Use the time now to think about the new start to come, but don't act yet. Consider your own spirituality.

Line meanings

Line 1

One should not perpetuate the affair.
Despite gossip, blessing will come.

When it looks as if an argument is about to develop, shut up and distance yourself from the other party and the problem. This may cause initial problems, but all will be well in the end.

Line 2

If one cannot engage in conflict
Then give way. Remain free of guilt.

This follows on from the previous line. Everyone will benefit by you remaining placid and backing away. You will feel a lot better by so doing.

Line 3

Contemplate ancient virtue. Persevere.
If you serve a ruler, seek not works.

Follow the ancient ways. You have learnt much and have used the wisdom well. Don't go after things which have been lost. Let them go. If you are working for someone, don't take on new responsibilities.

Line 4

If one cannot engage in conflict against the weak,
one should turn back.

Changing one's attitude, one finds peace.
Persevere this way.

Be prepared to stand your ground, but also to withdraw from any argumentative situation. Don't change your mind. All will be well.

Line 5

If one is in the right, seek an arbiter.
To contend brings good fortune.

You can trust a third party to give good advice. If you are right and true, things will go well for you.

Line 6

One has triumphed. One is decorated.
One's happiness is short-lived.

To win the battle does not mean to win the war. Similar conflicts will arise again in the future.

(7) Shih – The Army

Other keywords: Military/soldiers/group action.

Component trigrams: Water below, Earth above.

Modern meaning: If you command respect, you will receive support. Promotion is likely but with a battle. Some guidance will be given.

INTERPRETATION

An army is only as good as the people in it. It leaps into action when necessary, but not before. This hexagram concerns discipline, order and power.

JUDGEMENT

> The army needs steadfast discipline,
> Perseverance and a strong man to unite.

To be successful, any battalion needs a good leader who will unite the troops and bring them to order. The leader must command unlimited support, sincerity and enthusiasm, and make sure that justice and ultimately peace prevail. The hexagram suggests that you must find support and help from around you and that these friends must act together with you for the best interest.

IMAGE

> As the earth shelters waters within it,
> So does a wise ruler increase his wealth,
> By generosity towards his people.

It is necessary to be a kind, strong and supportive ruler. The respect of the nation depends on this. The ruler must educate the people in the correct manner.

LINE MEANINGS

LINE 1

> An army must set forth in proper order.
> If the order is not good, misfortune.

Order is vital to win the battle. Double check your plans. Look at your motives with honesty.

Line 2

The leader of the army is decorated.

You receive some honour or award. It is well deserved because those around you respect your work and judgement. Everyone shares in the honour because you share with them.

Line 3

Too many ride in the wagon. Misfortune.

Don't forget that you have certain weaknesses. If you do, failure will result. Exercise authority over yourself and others, as they may not be what they seem.

Line 4

The army retreats. No blame.

Sometimes it is necessary to retreat from a situation. Now is that time. It is not capitulation, but withdrawing for better advantage in the future. The situation will change with time, but don't force the pace.

Line 5

An enemy invades. Let the eldest lead.

It is necessary to be mature in order to win through. Immaturity will lead to failure. Not only are you still immature, so are your advisers. Beware. Look for people who have wisdom, not just age.

Line 6

The king rewards merit with position.
Small people he does not employ.

Success has been achieved. Look at what you have achieved. Have you merely become as bad as those you sought to displace? Maybe you don't deserve position and glory. Only the strong survive. It is survival of the fittest, and that may not be you.

(8) Pi – Union

Other keywords: Accord/holding together/seeking union/assistance.

Component trigrams: Earth below, Water above.

Modern meaning: Sharing experiences creates strong bonds. Help others and try to help yourself. Harmony in partnerships is indicated.

Interpretation

If you find someone with whom you share a strong bond, you will find someone who is prepared to give help whenever needed. If you don't feel this or sense it, the timing is wrong.

Judgement

> Holding together brings blessing.
> Do you possess the sublimity, constancy,
> And perseverance to be the centre of union?

Groups formed with a common bond stay together, as do relationships and any other partnership. Do you have the strength for this? Make up your mind quickly, in case the offer is withdrawn.

Image

> As waters over the earth flow together,
> So a wise ruler cultivates relationships.

Everyone must work towards the same ends for a group to achieve

its aims. Make sure your aims fit in with the group. Let yourself get close to the others.

Line meanings

Line 1

>
> Holding together depends on sincerity.
> Sincerity is like a full earthen bowl.
> Hold to him in truth and honesty.

You must be sincere in your undertakings. You must also be flexible. Make sure you are sympathetic with others.

Line 2

>
> Inner loyalty. But do not lose yourself.

Look at your motives again. You must be sincere. Don't agree just for the sake of it. Stick to your course.

Line 3

>
> Holding together with the wrong people.

You are with the wrong group. Withdraw. You can still remain friends from a distance. If you don't do this, you won't be free for later relationships.

Line 4

>
> When one may also show outward loyalty.

You can show your true feelings now. Be consistent and true to yourself, and don't let go of your own aims.

Line 5

>
> He holds together those who hold him.

If someone doesn't want to be a part of your group, you can't force them. People should come to you because they want to, not because they have to.

Lıne 6

One misses the right moment. Misfortune.

He who hesitates is lost. Decide on the necessary action and do it.

(9) Ȟsıao Ch'u — Tamıng foRce

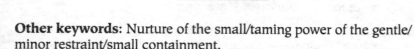

Other keywords: Nurture of the small/taming power of the gentle/minor restraint/small containment.

Component trigrams: Heaven below, Wind above.

Modern meaning: Clear away any small blockages in your path to prepare for the future. Be thankful for small mercies. Times may be difficult. Restraint is called for.

InteRpRetatıon

The signs of success are there, but nothing is happening right now. To be successful, you must also be flexible. Power and strength are needed, but so are sincerity and regard for other people.

Judgement

> The power of gentleness has success:
> Although it can give no rain,
> It drives and shapes great clouds.

It is necessary to move some obstacles to get a clear shot at goal. You do this by being friendly yet strong. This hexagram is all about strength with gentleness.

Image

> As the gentle wind shapes the clouds,
> So the wise man refines his bearing.

Use this waiting period to shape yourself. Look at yourself through the eyes of others, and make adjustments where necessary, not only to outward things such as appearance but also to your behaviour.

Line meanings

Line 1

> To return to one's station is no mistake.

If you can't achieve what you set out to do right now, leave it.

Line 2

> One allows oneself to be drawn back.
> Thus does one not lose oneself.

Other people who were following similar goals have retreated, and perhaps you need to follow their example.

Line 3

> Forcible advance. Failure and contention.

Pushing forward now would lead to failure. You are inclined to try to force other people against their will. You seem at odds with everyone. Don't be so aggressive.

Line 4

> If one is sincere, danger vanishes.

Others around you are sensing change. Follow their example and act now. Not to do so would be a mistake.

LINE 5

> If you are sincere and loyal
> Then you are rich in your neighbour.

Partnerships are favoured. You complement each other well. You have good friends. Recognise this.

LINE 6

> Success secured bit by bit. Be cautious.

When it seems likely that everything will fall into place, be on your guard. Don't make presumptions. Don't get tied down with something which would stifle you.

(10) Lu – TREADING CAREFULLY

Other keywords: Treading/conduct/comportment/caution.

Component trigrams: Marsh below, Heaven above.

Modern meaning: Stick to your guns. Don't hesitate. Press forward.

INTERPRETATION

This hexagram is all about harmony between the weak and the strong. They can work side by side without any ill effects to either. You should realise this, and try not to feel so superior all the time.

Don't be so isolationist. Others view you as rude. Try to do something about this.

Judgement

> One treads on the tail of a tiger.
> It does not bite. Success.

Things may be hard, but by being polite yet firm, pleasant yet strong, you will succeed.

Image

> Heaven above, lake below: discrimination.
> Thus a wise ruler reassures his people.

Whilst some people are higher in rank than others, they do not discriminate. Everyone has respect for each other.

Line meanings

Line 1

> Simple conduct. Progress without blame.

Opportunities for advancement are given. It is up to you to choose whether to accept these or not.

Line 2

> Treading a smooth, level way. Persevere.

Things are going well for you, even though they may not be for others. Keep on your path. Don't get involved in personal conflicts.

Line 3

> A lame man can tread on a tiger's tail.
> The tiger will bite him. Danger.
> A one-eyed man can see, but clearly?

If you think yourself above disaster, you will fail. Don't be blind to situations.

LINE 4

> If one is cautious and circumspect
> One can tread on the tail of a tiger.

Things are difficult, but not hopeless. Be cautious yet strong in purpose and you will win through.

LINE 5

> Resolute conduct. Be wary.

You must still be cautious and be aware of potential pitfalls. Keep going in the same direction and prepare for problems.

LINE 6

> Review your conduct. Weigh its effects.

You have completed your task, and now you look back to see whether what you have achieved is what you anticipated. People are judged by the fruit of their labours, and how they have acted.

(11) T'AI — TRANQUILLITY

Other keywords: Peace/contentment/success.

Component trigram: Heaven below, Earth above.

Modern meaning: Good fortune and harmony surround you. Share it with others. Plan for the future. Don't be rash. Progress steadily.

INTERPRETATION

Peace surrounds you. Everything is well. Everything is in order. This hexagram is all about strength within and peace without. It is also about seasons and time.

JUDGEMENT

> Peace means union, interrelation.
> As the small departs, the great approaches.
> Strength is within: the yielding is without.
> In this way does each receive its due.

Cultivation of a calm approach and way of behaviour is open to all, should they wish to find it. Anxieties are then forgotten and everything is harmony.

IMAGE

> As heaven and earth unite in due season,
> So the wise ruler divides and completes.
> He furthers and regulates
> The gifts of heaven and earth.
> Thus does he aid his people.

Time is divided into minutes, hours, days, months and seasons. The farmer adjusts the seasons to suit his needs. Working with nature rather than against it is the only way forward.

LINE MEANINGS

LINE 1

> Peace. One can direct one's will outward.
> Inner affinities lead to undertakings.

Legge's translation refers to picking wild flowers, and the grass coming with it. Other people with the same aims and goals will be attracted to you right now. Accept them.

Line 2

> Forbearing; resolved; vigilant; impartial:
> Thus can one find the way of the middle.

There are four ways to overcome difficulties and these are listed here. Undertake problems in these ways, irrespective of whether they be work related or personal.

Line 3

> Enjoy good fortune whilst it lasts.

Things change. Make the most of the situation now. Keep going but be aware that things won't always be this good. Don't get upset that things may change. It is only natural.

Line 4

> He comes down to meet his neighbour:
> Not boasting his wealth, but in sincerity.

Don't put yourself above others and adopt airs and graces which do not become you. You have no worries and should be at ease with yourself. This will cause you to be at ease with others. Be sincere.

Line 5

> A King's daughter marries. True modesty.

Legge's translation refers to Prince Yi and his daughters, who were to obey their husbands irrespective of their status at court. Be modest.

Line 6

> Peace ends. Ruin is at hand. Withdraw.

The situation has begun to change as expected, because you have kept your life in pigeon holes, allowing no interaction between

different spheres. Don't resist change. Back off a little and wait. You are vulnerable. Accept what fate has dished out.

(12) P'I – STAGNATION

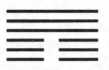

Other keywords: Disjunction/standstill/obstacles/obstruction.

Component trigrams: Earth below, Heaven above.

Modern meaning: Don't force the pace. Wait even if you think the rewards are there. Things will change. Be modest in everything.

INTERPRETATION

It may be difficult to keep to your path, but do so. This hexagram is the opposite of the previous.

JUDGEMENT

> The great departs, the small approaches.
> Evil people do not further a wise man,
> So he withdraws and remains steadfast.

Confusion and disorder are all around. Stick to your principles, even if it means withdrawing. There may be those around you with ill intent, probably of a materialistic nature. Keep away from them.

IMAGE

> When heaven and earth do not unite,
> The wise man turns to his inner worth.
> He does not permit himself to be honoured.

Don't get involved in things just because they seem glamorous.

Line meanings

Line 1

> One withdraws to save oneself.
> In steadfastness one finds blessing.

Legge's translation here is the same as for the first line of the previous hexagram. Sometimes you can only achieve success by withdrawing. Don't get involved in things which are none of your concern. Keep to yourself.

Line 2

> Standstill helps the great man:
> He brings blessing, even to the small.

Being involved with materialistic people is sometimes necessary and you have been true to yourself and your path so far by remaining aloof and not letting others affect you. Carry on this way.

Line 3

> When small people come to bear shame,
> This marks a turn for the better.

There are always people who rise in rank and status through foul means rather than fair. This line suggests that they know this inwardly. Could this be you?

Line 4

> He who acts at the command of heaven
> Is blessed. So are those with him.

You must exercise authority to proceed. You may not succeed in your endeavours but go ahead anyway, and others may well come to your aid.

Line 5

As standstill gives way: great caution

Things start to move. Be cautious, and don't be too sure of yourself. Pride comes before a fall. Look at yourself.

Line 6

Effort brings standstill to its end.

Movement occurs, but with a little help. Things are getting better.

(13) T'ung Jen – Companionship

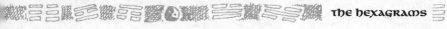

Other keywords: Society/fellowship/union of people.

Component trigrams: Sun below, Heaven above.

Modern meaning: Working with others brings rewards when everyone is working at their allotted task. Travel is indicated. Share with others.

Interpretation

This hexagram contains only one yin line, and it is this line which holds the others together, although they essentially appear to be the stronger. This hexagram is seen to be the complement of Shih or The Army.

Judgement

> Fellowship in the open leads to success.
> Great undertakings are favoured.
> A steadfast enlightened leader is needed.

To win through requires clarity of thought, strength of purpose and a fellowship with others. It is necessary to adopt all these qualities to succeed.

Image

> Heaven with fire: strength with clarity.
> As the lights in heaven arrange time,
> So the wise man organises society.

Order is essential in all things. This follows on from the judgement. If there are things which need tidying, organising or sorting, this should be done now. Maybe this could also indicate a fresh look at an existing relationship.

Line meanings

Line 1

Open fellowship begins without a gate.

You have joined together with others who share a common interest or bond. Stay with the group. Be open. Don't put up barriers.

Line 2

Fellowship within cliques: Humiliation

Don't limit yourself to a few friends. Open up your social circles. You only limit yourself if you limit your friendships.

Line 3

Fellowship that changes to mistrust.

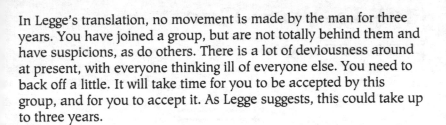

In Legge's translation, no movement is made by the man for three years. You have joined a group, but are not totally behind them and have suspicions, as do others. There is a lot of deviousness around at present, with everyone thinking ill of everyone else. You need to back off a little. It will take time for you to be accepted by this group, and for you to accept it. As Legge suggests, this could take up to three years.

Line 4

> Fellowship that comes forth from trouble,
> For trouble brings one to one's senses.

You are waiting for conflicts, but they aren't there, and you feel stupid because you have misjudged the situation and other people. Sometimes it is good to be wrong. You can't possibly be right all the time and in every situation.

Line 5

> Men bound in fellowship weep then laugh.
> First they struggle, then comes meeting.

The group you are in is strong and well structured. Sometimes you feel apart from the group, but there are many common bonds. Don't be so anxious. Accept the responsibilities of being part of the group, for it is a good thing to belong.

Line 6

> Fellowship amongst neighbours. No blame.

This line is about brotherhood between all peoples. Neighbours may not share your views and passions, but they are friends all the same. Maybe you should seek some common ground with them. Look also at your relationships with people of different backgrounds, colours, creeds and sex.

(14) Ta Yu – Great Possession

Other keywords: Wealth/abundance.

Component trigrams: Heaven below, Fire above.

Modern meaning: Success is assured. Work and study for the future. Things look favourable.

Interpretation

This hexagram is all about a kind ruler who is surrounded by strong and willing helpers. He is modest, kind and unselfish. He has inner strength but a clarity of mind to be able to see the need for harmony with those around him.

Judgement

When strength and clarity unite:
A time of blessing: of strength within;
Of enlightenment and culture without.
The yielding receives the honoured place;
He is firm and strong, ordered and clear.

Firmness and strength are vital to succeed. Mental clarity and order are also equally important. All attributes must live in harmony one with the other. A ruler who has all these things will receive honour.

Image

As the sun sheds light on good and evil,
So the wise man curbs evil and furthers good.
He thereby fulfils the will of heaven.

Evil must be vanquished in order for good to rule. Likewise must mankind strive for this ultimate goal.

Line meanings

Line 1

Keeping away from what is harmful;
Keeping mindful of difficulties to come.

When accumulating power and possessions, it is a temptation to compromise yourself. Watch out for this. Difficulties are yet to come and you must be careful to guard against arrogance and being overbearing.

Line 2

A big wagon will carry a heavy load:
A wise man relies on able helpers

Be flexible and be prepared to move should the need arise. Don't let your possessions become restrictions. Others are able to help you if you let them.

Line 3

A prince offers his wealth to heaven:
A wise man offers his to his prince.
A petty man cannot do this.

Share your good fortune with others. If you keep your wealth to yourself, it will become a restriction. Giving is often better than receiving – dwell on this thought.

LINE 4

> One is different from one's neighbour.
> If one is poorer, one must shun envy;
> If one is richer, then possess modestly.

Don't be envious of others, as they are not envious of you. Be modest. Don't try to keep up with the Joneses – it's not worth it.

LINE 5

> He who makes his truth accessible,
> Yet is dignified, is favoured indeed.

You make friends by being sincere, not by being pushy. Be dignified by all means, but be aware of others, be unselfish and accept others as they accept you.

LINE 6

> He is blessed by heaven. All goes well.

As a direct result of remaining modest, sincere and honourable, the man has received the blessings of heaven. You may meet such a person. Share his good fortune with him and learn.

(15) Ch'ien – Humility

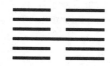

Other keywords: Modesty.

Component trigrams: Mountain below, Earth above.

Modern meaning: If you remain modest, others will give you the help you need. It is vital to remain tolerant of others. Seek harmony at all costs.

Interpretation

Balance is necessary. Modesty knows no class barriers, no limits. Cultivate it if you wish to grow.

Judgement

> He who possesses something great
> Must not make it too full.
> Things are easy for the modest person.

Fairness, sincerity and humility make a good person. Nobody likes the boaster or the bigot. Make sure you are not one of the latter group.

Image

> Within the earth, a mountain. Inner wealth.
> Thus, the wise ruler reduces fullness
> And augments that which is too little.
> He weighs things and makes them equal.

Extremes are unwise. Compromise is better.

Line meanings

Line 1

> A wise man is modest about his modesty.
> Thus he accomplishes difficult things.

If you are living in harmony, are modest and sincere, you can take on any endeavour, knowing it will meet with success. If, however, there is conflict or anxiety surrounding you, now is not the time to act.

Line 2

> Modest in heart, modest in manner.

Responsibilities are given to those people who are modest in character. The way you behave shows your inner self. People see you for what you are.

LINE 3

A man of merit who also is modest
Can carry things through to conclusion.

Fame brings its own rewards. However, don't allow the fame and recognition you have achieved to make you big-headed or immodest. If you remain modest, you will be loved and supported.

LINE 4

Modesty prompts action, not inaction.

Accept responsibilities given to you. Don't shy away from work, and don't look for excuses for inaction. Other people depend on you and you cannot let them down. You have responsibilities to them also.

LINE 5

Modesty expressed in forcefulness.

Sometimes you have to be forceful to make improvements. Modesty does not mean weakness. Remember to be objective. You may be asked to do something. Think about consulting a friend.

LINE 6

Modesty expressed in self-discipline.

Immodesty leads to conflict, even between good friends. Look at yourself and rectify any problems there. Win back friendships by returning to the correct way.

Note Ch'ien is also the name for hexagram no. 1, although the actual hexagram drawing and the meaning are totally different.

(16) Yu – Happiness

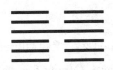

Other keywords: Enthusiasm/joy/harmony/bliss.

Component trigrams: Earth below, Thunder above.

Modern meaning: Try to advertise yourself and your capabilities more, but don't believe your own publicity. Plan for the future, and remember that wealth doesn't necessarily bring happiness. Spiritual matters are favoured above the material.

Interpretation

You inspire enthusiasm in yourself and others. This is an action hexagram, sparking devotion from within.

Judgement

> Enthusiasm: movements of inherent harmony.
> A great time indeed. One needs helpers.

Being at one with those around you leads to success. If you are enthusiastic, those around you will be too.

Image

> As thunder resounds out of the earth,
> So kings of old made music in the temple
> To honour merit and devote it to God.
> A time for song and dance. A time for awe.

Remembering the spirituality of God and of yourself leads to harmony and happiness.

LINE MEANINGS

LINE 1

Enthusiasm that boasts. Misfortune.

Don't be arrogant or boastful. Others find you boring and seek to distance themselves from you.

LINE 2

Be correct in a time of enthusiasm.
Persevere in inner steadfastness.
To be ready to withdraw is prudent.

Don't be misled by fantasy. Don't crawl to the boss or neglect those below you. Be self-reliant and keep to your way. Hold back a little if necessary, and be prepared to distance yourself from any misguided enthusiasm in others.

LINE 3

Enthusiasm that looks upward. Regrets.
Hesitation can also bring remorse.

Don't be dazzled by those in a higher position than you and wait on their every word before taking any action. If the time seems right to act, do so. Above all, remember self-reliance.

LINE 4

The source of enthusiasm achieves much:
He gathers friends as hair in the clasp.

You are admired by others who see you as honest and sincere. If you support other people, they will return the favour.

LINE 5

Obstructed enthusiasm. Frustration.
Persistently ill: still he does not die.

Pressures are all around and you feel hemmed in. Sometimes we need this pressure to spur us on.

Line 6

> Deluded enthusiasm. How can this last?
> But to awake from delusion: no blame.

You are caught up in your own enthusiasm and ego. It is necessary to come down to earth a little and see the reality of situations. This will help you in the future.

(17) Sui – following

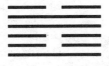

Other keywords: Pursuit.

Component trigrams: Thunder below, Marsh above.

Modern meaning: Let others take charge for now. Avoid conflict. Be flexible. Relax. Keep your goals in mind.

Interpretation

Happiness binds people together. The weak will always follow the strong. When you are happy, sometimes it is as well to follow, as no harm can come of it.

Judgement

> In following, be steadfast and consistent;
> If one would be one who is followed,
> One must first follow in the right.

To be successful, sometimes you must lead by example. To create a following by immoral means will result in failure.

ImAGE

> As thunder withdraws to its winter rest,
> So too, the wise man allows himself rest.
> He follows and looks to the laws of nature.

Be flexible and learn to adapt to changing situations rather than trying to resist.

LINE mEANINGS

LINE 1

> As times change, one must adapt.
> One must not lose oneself. Persevere.

Listen to other people. Accept their views and be less solitary. You must be open-minded and less blinkered, and widen your social circle to include people who may not be in your immediate group, even if it seems likely that this will bring conflict.

LINE 2

> If one clings to the weak,
> One loses the strong.

Choose your friends carefully. Weed out those amongst your group who are untrustworthy.

LINE 3

> If one clings to the strong,
> One loses the weak.

Choose the way in which you want to go, and the friends with whom you wish to share this. There is a need for self-analysis here. Don't be swayed by others.

Line 4

> Followed by flatterers. Be sincere.

When you have reached a position of authority, many people will flatter you without sincerity on their part. Don't be taken in, and watch your ego. You are responsible for the people you have around you. Make your intentions clear.

Line 5

> One follows the good with sincerity.

If you stay true to yourself and your path, you will succeed. Let the light guide you.

Line 6

> A king's firm allegiance
> Can bring back even the sage.

Ask someone wise to help you with what you wish to do. You will both benefit.

(18) Ku – Disruption

Other keywords: Fixing/work on what has been spoiled/poison.

Component trigrams: Wind below, Mountain above.

Modern meaning: Honesty will pay dividends. Think hard. Press forward with care. Rectify mistakes.

INTERPRETATION

Dishonesty surrounds you. Try to be more honest. Try also to be more objective and clear. The Chinese character for this hexagram concerns a rotting bowl in which worms are breeding. Things have been spoiled.

JUDGEMENT

> Removing corruption promises success.
> If one deliberates with great care,
> Before and after the starting point,
> Then great undertakings are favoured.

To rectify problems and prevent further decay, we must find the root cause of the problems. Action is necessary. It is necessary to be less lethargic and weak.

IMAGE

> As a wind, blowing low on a mountain,
> Thus does the wise man remove corruption.
> As a wind, he first stirs up the people.
> As a mountain, he gives them nourishment.

This clearly refers to the component trigrams. It refers to the help others can give if orders are clear and aims are honest.

LINE MEANINGS

LINE 1

> Lay no blame upon one's forebears
> In reforming what rigidity has spoiled.

It is time to change your principles. Things have changed and you must change with them. Consider your new stance carefully, as it will have far-reaching effects.

Line 2

> In reforming what inner weakness has spoiled
> One must not be too persistent.

It takes time to make changes, and you must be patient. Try to understand that other people may also have difficulties with which to contend. Don't go to extremes. Take the middle way.

Line 3

> One reforms what has been spoiled:
> A little remorse, but no great blame.

Energy is necessary to make changes, and other people are annoyed at the pace at which you are working. However, this is a case where the end will justify the means.

Line 4

> Tolerating decay leads to humiliation.

Action is imperative. Don't let things drift. Try to be less indecisive. Face up to the problems and do something now. Things may get worse before they get better.

Line 5

> One sets things right with able helpers.
> One's reforms meet with praise.

Other people know that you are to blame for your situation, and will praise you when they realise that you are trying to do something about this. They may try to help.

Line 6

> He serves not kings and princes;
> The sage sets himself higher goals.

Remember you are working for the future. Don't dwell on past problems and relationships which have not worked out. Concentrate more on things which give happiness. Look at yourself and your motives. Work for the future, not only for yourself, but for others.

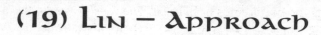

(19) Lin – Approach

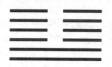

Other keywords: Conduct/becoming great/advance/authority.

Component trigrams: Marsh below, Earth above.

Modern meaning: Advance slowly and with care. Consider others more. Make the most of your good fortune, as everything is short-lived. Rash decisions are costly now.

Interpretation

This hexagram means 'becoming great and powerful'. It is a hexagram of growth and strength. Keeping to the course is indicated. Things will change soon, in the same way as one season makes way for the next.

Judgement

> A time of joyous progress brings favour.
> One should persevere in the right
> For its end will surely come.

This hexagram is about approaching spring and the regeneration this brings to the world. Making sure our aims and motives are just is the only thing right now.

Image

> As a lake is deep: as the earth is broad:
> So is the wise man in his will to teach.

There are no limits, no boundaries or barriers. The wise person will realise this also applies to learning, and seek to help others with their learning through his vast knowledge.

Line meanings

Line 1

Joint approach. Persevere in the right.

You are in tune with circumstances and things are going well. Keep going, but don't get carried away.

Line 2

Joint approach. A call from above.

Remember that you have to address both your material side and your spiritual side. Things of the earth have a limited life.

Line 3

An easy-going approach brings harm.
If one is induced to regret it,
Then one becomes free of blame.

Don't be overconfident or blasé. Think about your attitude and rectify any faults there. Others may be experiencing problems. Be caring towards them.

Line 4

The complete approach:
To draw up another with one.

People who may be outside your social group will now feature in your life, and become friends. Be sympathetic and help.

Line 5

The wise approach.
This is right for a great prince.

Select others to help you with care. Let them get on with the work you have given them without your interference. Remember they rely on you in the same way as you rely on them.

LINE 6

The great-hearted approach.
The approach of a sage brings blessing.

You may have withdrawn from the material and concentrated on the spiritual. Now is the time to use what you have learned from this isolation and rejoin the material world.

(20) KUAN — OBSERVING

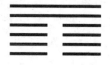

Other keywords: Contemplation/view surveillance.

Component trigrams: Earth below, Wind above.

Modern meaning: Think about future plans. Look more deeply at things. Work with others. Listen and learn.

INTERPRETATION

'See and be seen' is the main message of this hexagram. Be an example to others for them to follow. You command respect.

JUDGEMENT

The ablution has been made
But not yet the offering.
Full of trust, they look up to him.

Ablution refers to an ancient Chinese tradition of cleansing. This hexagram is all about Tao and the way. Past, present and future are all within sight.

Image

As the wind goes everywhere over the earth
And the grasses bend before its power;
So the wise ruler goes everywhere
And the people are swayed, as grass by the wind.

People respect and are loyal to the King because he takes the time and trouble to be seen and to see. He is not isolationist, but is seen to take an interest in those around him.

Line meanings

Line 1

Childlike contemplation:
For the small man, no blame;
For the wise man, humiliation.

It is necessary to understand others and their actions in order to be considered wise. Look at realities and not at pageant and fantasy.

Line 2

Contemplation through one's doorway.

Peering through a spyhole leads to a limited view. Your view is also limited. If you are happy with this, so be it. However, maybe you should consider taking a broader overall view.

Line 3

Self-contemplation: to decide one's way.

It is necessary to look at yourself from the outsider's viewpoint. Consider all the aspects of yourself and your direction before deciding which direction to follow.

Line 4

> Contemplating the light of the kingdom.
> He exerts influence as the king's guest.

If you have learned from the past, you are likely to be given a position of authority or should try to achieve a higher position yourself.

Line 5

> Self-contemplation: to judge oneself.

If others respect you, you must command their respect and be above fault. Look at yourself and make sure you are satisfied with what you see. If you have been looking inwardly too much of late, maybe now is the time to make your judgement, rather than continuing the period of introspection.

Line 6

> The selfless contemplation of life.

You have now finished your inner contemplation. Remember the past, as there is a danger that you will forget it and make similar mistakes. If you stand outside the ways of the world, you will find peace. If, however, you are still contemplating it, you have yet to find this peace.

(21) Shih Ho – Biting Through

Other keywords: Chewing/judging.

Component trigrams: Thunder below, Fire above.

Modern meaning: Remain positive about your successes. Legal matters may arise. Don't let other people get you down through their own negativities. You can win.

Interpretation

This hexagram concerns biting through obstacles, overcoming problems and disharmony, thwarting petty jealousies and overcoming legal problems.

Judgement

> Biting through has success
> When unity cannot be established.

It is necessary to remove obstacles immediately so as to prevent further damage. However, this must be done correctly.

Image

> Thunder and lightning: clarity and fear.
> Thus kings of old made firm the laws
> And clearly defined the penalties.

Fairness, order and clarity are necessary to be correct. It is necessary to have a clear code of conduct and clear penalties for those who don't follow the way.

Line meanings

Line 1

> At first, a light punishment. No blame.

Initial crimes need softer sentences than further crimes. This line suggests that the incorrect things you have so far done are not irreversible. If you change course now, no harm will come.

Line 2

> Biting soft food, one buries one's nose:
> In anger, one goes a little too far.

Other people are being so unfair on you that you are inclined to dish out punishment which is far too hard. You feel your actions are justified. Maybe they are.

Line 3

> To bite old meat; to lack authority;
> Either will bring one some humiliation.

Legge's translation refers to biting into something rotten. You know that you must do something now. There will be conflict, and you may not come out in the best light. You may feel humiliated. Don't keep on about old issues (old meat). Let it drop.

Line 4

> Biting dry grisly meat: big obstacles.
> Be as a metal arrow: hard and straight.

Be hard and you will win through. There are lots of obstacles now. You can succeed only with a firm and positive stance. Your enemies are strong and you will have to be likewise.

Line 5

> Biting lean meat: clear but not easy.
> Be like yellow gold: true but impartial.

The situation is clear. That doesn't make it easy. Keep to your mettle and don't back down when dealing with opponents. You can sometimes be too easy-going with others. Be steadfast.

Line 6

> He covers his ears with his own yoke:
> He becomes deaf to warnings. Misfortune.

The offender, who may be you, is obstinate, incorrigible and arrogant. If this is you, take the necessary steps to change.

(22) Pi – Adornment

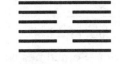

Other keywords: Ornament/grace/beauty.

Component trigrams: Fire below, Mountain above.

Modern meaning: Make an impression, but make sure you live within your means. There are things to sort out still, but make only small changes. The time is not right.

Interpretation

Beauty and harmony are important. This is the hexagram of the artist and of the lover of beautiful things. It is also about how others see you, and whether they see you in the light in which you would wish to be seen.

Judgement

> Grace means adornment, beauty of form.
> Graceful form is right in small matters.

Whilst external adornment is pleasant to the eye, it is only an external thing, and must be used sparingly. The combination of love and justice leads to the formation of rules. However good they are in theory, however, they are only as effective as those who issue them.

Image

> Clarity within and quiet without:
> The wise man has time for meditation.

Contemplation brings about tranquillity but may not necessarily change the will. Free will and choice remain no matter what.

Line meanings

Line 1

One leaves the carriage and walks.

Opportunities are around you. Sometimes when an easy option is offered, it is better to take the harder route. Other people will appreciate this quality in you if you choose to adopt it.

Line 2

He preens his beard.
It wags with his chin.

You try to cultivate the things about you which others find pleasing. This changes your appearance and also your character. Don't be vain, and don't try to change things just to create the right impression on others.

Line 3

He who has grace must still persevere.

Accept the good things in life, but don't go over the top. If you become greedy and avaricious, you will ultimately lose out. Be careful.

Line 4

Grace or simplicity? One must be true.

You have a full social calendar. Other people seem to like your company. Are you being true to yourself, however? Maybe the time is right to reduce your social engagements and spend time with your real friends rather than with hangers-on.

Line 5

One seeks grace in the heights,
But one's gift is meagre. Humiliation.
Yet if one is sincere, one will be blessed.

By reducing your social engagements, and being less materialistic, you find a true friend, one with whom you can find yourself. This makes you feel humble and awkward. His sincerity is genuine. He will make a good friend.

LINE 6

Simple grace. No blame.

When you are really great, you don't need trappings or external adornment. Grace is simplicity. This is true happiness.

Note: Pi is also the name for hexagram 8. The meaning, though, is entirely different.

(23) Po – Stripping Away

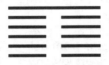

Other keywords: Collapse/splitting up/disintegration/hacking.

Component trigrams: Earth below, Mountain above.

Modern meaning: Don't act now. The odds are not in your favour. Things will change and disruption will occur. Wait.

INTERPRETATION

There is a lack of balance and harmony. To do anything now would put you in a weak position, so wait until things change. Take no action whatsoever.

JUDGEMENT

At a time of disintegration of the good,
The wise man undertakes nothing.

When inferior people are making all the headway, it is wiser to stay in the background and do nothing.

Image

> As a mountain rests, depends, on the earth,
> So those above ensure their position
> Only by giving generously to those below.

Things only stay when they are broad and firm, rather than narrow and lacking in strong foundation. Giving to other people is a good thing.

Line meanings

Line 1

> Splitting apart begins from below.
> Do not persist in open loyalty.

Other people are trying to undermine you. Wait and take no action. If you act now, you will fail.

Line 2

> Splitting apart mounts upward. Danger.
> Do not persist in proclaiming a view.

You have not heeded the warning given in the first line, and are likely to fail. You feel isolated and nobody seems there to help you. Be careful.

Line 3

> He splits from evil. Isolation. No blame.

Leading on from the last line, the isolation continues. You decide to compromise with those causing problems. This is acceptable.

Line 4

The splitting comes to one's own self.

Not a good line. It indicates total defeat and failure. You must put up with this. You can do nothing.

Line 5

Forces are changed and favour comes.

You take action. Things will improve financially and the situation will be a lot easier. Someone may try to help you.

Line 6

As fruit falls and splits to give new seed:
So good will arise, and evil be split apart.

You have suffered a lot. Things have changed beyond recognition, and not totally for the better. You must accept the change, and make something of it. Others will help you. Don't be unhappy. What has happened is in the past. Don't dwell on it, as it can't be changed.

(24) fu — Returning

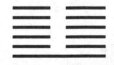

Other keywords: Turning point.

Component trigrams: Thunder below, Earth above.

Modern meaning: Timing must be cultivated. Patience is needed. New energies will appear. Be cautious, as with anything new.

INTERPRETATION

Improvements all round. Things will change with the seasons. This hexagram concerns winter and the start of a new yearly cycle.

JUDGEMENT

> Success comes in accord with the time.
> Friends forgather in harmony. No blame.
> Now is the time to undertake something.

A time of change for the better. Think about the future. Plan. Know what you want, and use the time of waiting to its best advantage.

IMAGE

> As thunder withdraws to its deepest rest,
> So kings of antiquity closed the passes;
> Merchants and strangers did not go about;
> Nor did the ruler travel the provinces.

The winter was considered a time of rest, in the same way as the growth of plants was arrested. Energy is being renewed. This can also be seen to be a period of recuperation after illness.

LINE MEANINGS

LINE 1

> Turn back early, before going too far.
> Thus one finds not remorse, but favour.

Don't allow yourself to do something you would later regret. Stick to your path. Put aside anything evil, untoward or which is against your principles.

Line 2

> Quiet return, guided by a good man.

Influential people are all around you. You feel a sense of a new start and are thinking of accepting an offer made.

Line 3

> Repeated returnings. Herein is danger.

Be careful. Keep going and don't lose faith and turn back. Stop being such a defeatist. You seem to fear reaching your goals. If you keep changing your mind and your plans, you will get nowhere.

Line 4

> Whilst walking in the midst of others
> One turns alone to follow the right way.

Someone you respect will help you. Others may feel that you have deserted them. You can't help that. Move onwards without guilt.

Line 5

> Noble-hearted return. No remorse.
> Thus does one test oneself.

When change presents itself, you must go with it. Other people will eventually see that you are doing the right thing and may choose to follow suit.

Line 6

> Missing the turning point: Misfortune.

You haven't taken the opportunities presented and they have now passed you by. You have stuck to your old routines because you feared the new. This has been a big mistake, as you have missed a golden opportunity. There's nothing you can do now, but wait for another opportunity to present itself. However, it won't be as good! The chances of recovery were there for you at that time. Such things come around again rarely.

(25) Wu WANG — CORRECTNESS

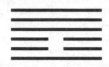

Other keywords: Without mistake/innocence/ the simple.

Component trigrams: Thunder below, Heaven above.

Modern meaning: Don't go beyond your limits. Be selfless and simple. Problems are only temporary. Be prepared.

INTERPRETATION

This hexagram concerns going with one's inner spirituality and according with the will of heaven. This is innocence, harmony and truth.

JUDGEMENT

> Innocence succeeds through perseverance.
> If one is not as one should be: misfortune.
> When innocence is gone, where can one go?

By keeping with the will of heaven, by retaining innocence, one is as one should be. When one is not innocent, failure results.

IMAGE

> As thunder rolls under heaven,
> And all things attain natural innocence,
> So kings of old fostered all beings.

The thunder brings rain. This in turn leads to creation of plant life. Wise people learn to work in harmony with nature.

Line meanings

Line 1

Innocent behaviour attains its will.

Trust your inner voice, your instincts. Good fortune will result.

Line 2

Count not on reaping whilst ploughing.
Thus should one undertake something.

If everything depends on you doing something now, it is better to wait. If, however, you are acting according to present trends and for no major gain, then go ahead.

Line 3

A passer-by takes one's tethered cow.

Bad luck and misfortune surround you. You learn to accept such events and put them down to fate. Your loss is another's gain.

Line 4

He who can persevere remains blameless.

Stick to your direction, irrespective of what other people might say. You know what is best for you.

Line 5

Take no medicine. One is not at fault.
The illness is from without:
It will pass of itself.

You have met with an accident, an illness or some other unplanned misfortune. You will recover in due course. Don't worry. Don't make it worse than it is by being anxious.

Line 6

When innocent action is wrong: wait.

Don't trust your instincts as you are likely to be wrong. Don't do anything at all. Wait.

(26) Ta Ch'u – Taming force

Other keywords: Containment/the taming power of the great.

Component trigrams: Heaven below, Mountain above.

Modern meaning: Work hard and expect slow progress. Success will come. Luck is on your side. Learn from the past.

Interpretation

This hexagram concerns inner power with outer calm. It is all about holding firm, sticking to one's guns, holding together, or holding back.

Judgement

> To be able to keep strength still;
> This is great correctness.
> Firm and strong, genuine and true.
> Daily does a wise man renew his virtue.
> Thus can great things be undertaken.

The wise ruler makes it a routine to strengthen his character daily by keeping still. It is favourable to enter anything to do with public life or social concern.

Image

> Within the mountain: heaven. Hidden riches.
> So the wise man studies the sayings of old
> And the deeds of the past to enrich himself.

Learning from past mistakes and from past successes makes a man successful in the future.

Line meanings

Line 1

> Danger is at hand. One should desist.
> Thus one does not endanger oneself.

If you push ahead now, things will go wrong. Wait a while.

Line 2

> When the restraining force overwhelms,
> Remove the wheels from your wagon.

When you find yourself in a position where you are the weaker, do nothing but wait. It is not defeat, but realism.

Line 3

> As good team horses pull together,
> Go forward thus, aware of dangers.
> Practise both driving and self-defence.

Keep going. You realise there will be problems and you must be prepared for them. Stick to your goal.

Line 4

> The dehorning of a young bull. Success.

If you act now, any threat of harm will be eliminated.

LINE 5

The tusk of a gelded boar. Good fortune.

The boar is dangerous, but when he has been gelded, his character is altered and he is less of a danger. Thus, if you do something now to change the nature of those who threaten you, the dangers will be lessened.

LINE 6

One attains the way of heaven. Success.

Things have gone well. You have achieved your aims.

(27) I – NOURISHMENT

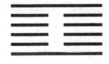

Other keywords: The corners of the mouth/cheeks.

Component trigrams: Thunder below, Mountain above.

Modern meaning: Watch not only what you eat and drink but what you say. Build up your strength and wait. Don't be over-ambitious.

INTERPRETATION

What you eat may not be what you think it is. Likewise, you may not be what you appear to be. Remember the saying, 'You are what you eat'. Remember, also your spiritual nourishment.

Judgement

> Pay heed to nourishing what is right
> And in what one seeks to nourish oneself.
> As heaven and earth nourish all beings,
> So a holy sage nourishes men of worth.
> Thereby, he reaches the whole people.

Look after those who need help. Remember also to take care of yourself. Consider carefully what you eat and drink.

Image

> Within the calm mountain, thunder stirs.
> As God comes forth in The Arousing,
> And perfects in tranquil Keeping Still,
> So is the wise man, tranquil in movement.

Watching what you say, and what you eat and drink, and being caring about yourself and others, leads to wisdom.

Line meanings

Line 1

> To envy others with drooping mouth,
> Is to let go one's self-reliance.

Legge's translation refers back to tortoise shells which were perhaps the original source of the patterns of yin and yang. This line talks about resentment and envy of others. Even though you have everything you need, you still want more. This is contemptible.

Line 2

> To accept support brings misfortune,
> If one deviates from self-reliance.

Why do you seek nourishment from other people when you are more than capable of providing your own? This is not a good thing.

LINE 3

> One turns away from true nourishment
> To desire, gratification, desire.
> One's way runs round and round. No goal.

You aren't taking care of yourself properly. You seem to have lost your way. No good comes from pursuit of pleasure for its own sake.

LINE 4

> To accept support brings good fortune:
> One seeks helpers like a hungry tiger.

You realise your responsibilities to yourself. Other people are needed to help you achieve your aims, and you must look for them. Take advantage of favourable opportunities.

LINE 5

> He deviates from self-reliance. Good.
> He should not undertake great things.

Be aware of your limitations. Find someone to help you. Don't attempt anything too much right now.

LINE 6

> The sage who nourishes brings blessing.

Your awareness of your own spirituality is a nourishment for you. Remember that you have more than others, and consider yourself fortunate. Things can and do change. Anything you undertake now for the good of others will be successful.

Note Hexagram 42 also has the same Chinese name, although the actual hexagram drawing and the meaning are totally different.

(28) Ta Kuo – Excess

Other keywords: Great heaviness/preponderance of the great/continuation.

Component trigrams: Wind below, Marsh above.

Modern meaning: Extraordinary action is called for now. Listen to your inner voice. Success is likely.

Interpretation

This hexagram has four strong inner lines and two weak outer lines. It is like a roof which has a strong centre but weak edge, and is a hexagram of caution and the necessity for change.

Judgement

> The weight of the great is excessive:
> The load too heavy; the support too weak.
> At a time of Great Heaviness
> It furthers one to have somewhere to go.

It is necessary to find a way to address the balance. There is some strength, but not enough.

Image

> As a lake rises above the treetops
> In extraordinary times of flood:
> So the wise man, in extraordinary times,
> Is unconcerned if he stands alone.

> Even if he has to renounce the world,
> He is as undaunted as joyousness.

The situation is only temporary. It may be necessary to isolate yourself for the time being.

LINE MEANINGS

LINE 1

> To spread rushes beneath is no mistake.

Be careful. Other people may suggest that you are being overly cautious, but take no notice. Protect yourself. If planning a new venture, make sure that you are setting down strong foundations.

LINE 2

> A dry poplar sprouts at the root.
> An older man takes a young wife. New life.

A new venture, a new love affair, a newly discovered spirituality. All this is indicated by this line. Things look promising.

LINE 3

> A beam sags to breaking point.

You haven't taken notice of the signs, nor have you exercised caution. Don't do anything. Stay put. To push forward now would be disastrous.

LINE 4

> The beam is braced. Good fortune.
> Any ulterior motives bring shame.

A helper has appeared. This has eased the situation. However, don't take advantage of this person. If you abuse his generosity, you will regret it.

Line 5

A withered poplar puts forth flowers.
A man takes an older wife. No renewal.

Don't give up friendships with others because you think they are beneath you. You now have so much going for you that you think they no longer have a part in your life. You are wrong. Your life hasn't changed that much.

Line 6

Swamped by circumstances. No blame.

You have fallen on bad times through your own enthusiasm and strength of purpose. You didn't see the signs. No great harm will come in the long term because you realise that this is all part of the learning process.

(29) K'an – The Deep

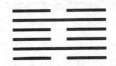

Other keywords: Abysmal/valleys/water/the perilous pit.

Component trigrams: Deep below, Deep above.

Modern meaning: Watch for pitfalls and take care. Conflict is likely. Proceed with caution but proceed. Have faith in yourself.

Interpretation

This hexagram is all about danger. The trigrams are the same, and both mean danger. Whether you live permanently with danger or not, the message is clear – caution but not standstill.

JUDGEMENT

> When danger is doubled, be true, sincere.
> He that is so has success in his heart.

When faced with danger, don't give up, but remain courageous, sincere and honest. These attributes will see you through. To stop would mean that you would be swamped and possibly go under.

IMAGE

> As water flows on, on, on to reach its goal
> So the wise man walks in lasting virtue.

If you try to stay blameless (i.e. above the water), you will win through.

LINE MEANINGS

LINE 1

> Repeated danger. One falls into the pit.
> One has lost one's way.

When permanently surrounded by danger, it is dangerous in itself to become blasé about it. Be careful not to fall into that pit. Keep your wits about you.

LINE 2

> In danger, strive for small things only.

Concentrate your energies on smaller projects rather than on anything large.

LINE 3

> Forward and backward. Abyss on abyss.
> When in a bog, pause at first and wait.

You can't win. Whatever you do seems wrong. Stop a while and consider matters. Use this temporary pause. Don't act now. To do so is folly.

Line 4

In lowly earthen vessels: wine and rice,
Presented most simply. No blame in this.

Your safety is secured by lowering your standards a little and accepting help from someone you may have considered beneath you. Be kind to those who have helped you. They act in sincerity and simplicity. Do likewise.

Line 5

Water fills an abyss, only to the rim.

Danger still lurks. Don't take on anything new or too large. Be simple in your thoughts and actions. You are likely to stretch yourself too far if you take on new projects now.

Line 6

Shut in by thorn-hedged prison walls;
For years one does not find the way.

All your problems have come home to roost. Be very careful. Look at your motives and see how they may have led to this situation. Resolve to put right the wrongs you see in yourself. You have brought all this about yourself.

(30) Li – Fire

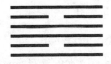

Other keywords: Clinging/shining.

Component trigrams: Fire below, Fire above.

Modern meaning: Recognising your limits brings success. Anything intellectual goes well. Be calm, yet firm.

Interpretation

This hexagram is the same above as below, and reinforces the message of fire. Fire is warm, bright, radiant and has no form of its own. It concerns standing in the light rather than the dark.

Judgement

> One can succeed only by perseverance.
> The care of one's cow brings one favour.

Stick with what you see to be correct and true. Make your aims clear as fire is clear. Cultivate docility like the cow.

Image

> The great man perpetuates his brightness
> And illuminates all quarters of the world

Spreading your light rather than hiding it is the message here.

Line meanings

Line 1

> At sunrise one's thoughts run criss-cross.

Make sure you stay on the straight and narrow. Remain consistent and composed. Don't allow yourself to be pushed into things about which you feel uneasy.

LINE 2

The yellow light of midday. Blessing.

Yellow was thought to be a colour of culture, balance and harmony. Things are going well. Make sure you maintain the balance.

LINE 3

At sunset, men either feast or sing,
Or bewail the shortness of life. Misfortune.

Old age brings with it thoughts of death and of mortality. To the wise man, these thoughts are not entertained. Death will come whether we worry about it or not. Don't worry about the future. It takes care of itself.

LINE 4

A meteor is bright, but soon is gone.
A straw fire flares quickly, but soon dies.

This line concerns the waste of resources. Don't waste your energies.

LINE 5

Tears and sighs. But lament brings blessing.

Others are worried about you because of the way you are behaving. Try to retain your clarity of mind and your humility. Keep pressing on with your plans, but be aware of the concern of others about your course.

LINE 6

True enlightenment: measured discipline

None of us is perfect. You realise you have certain imperfections in attitude and behaviour and have sought to do something about these. However, some faults still remain. These are harmless, but it is good that you are aware of them. Try to remember to be strong yet kind, especially when dealing with your rivals.

(31) Hsein – Sensitivity

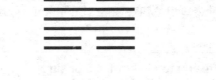

Other keywords: Influence/wooing/tension/stimulation.

Component trigrams: Mountain below, Marsh above.

Modern meaning: Be receptive to others and their ideas. Don't be envious. Change should be expected. Partnerships are strongly featured.

Interpretation

You are outwardly happy and content. You attract others who feel comfortable in your company. Be helpful towards others, but be genuine, and don't seek to be top dog at others' expense.

Judgement

Influence succeeds by perseverance.
Taking a maiden to wife brings favour.
To defer to the weaker brings peace.

Attractions are a two-way thing. Remember to remain inwardly calm, even if you feel outwardly ecstatic. Be considerate of your partner.

Image

At the top of the mountain, a lake.
Thus is the wise man ready to receive
By virtue of his emptiness.

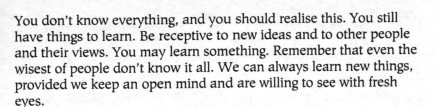

You don't know everything, and you should realise this. You still have things to learn. Be receptive to new ideas and to other people and their views. You may learn something. Remember that even the wisest of people don't know it all. We can always learn new things, provided we keep an open mind and are willing to see with fresh eyes.

Line meanings

Line 1

The inner stimulus to influence.

Making changes to yourself is necessary to progress. Others are yet to be aware of your desires to alter yourself. Maybe you need to make more major changes than you think.

Line 2

Dependent influence bodes ill. Wait.

Legge's translation refers to flexing the calves. You can only do this by standing still. Don't act now, as failure will result. Any changes you wish to make must wait.

Line 3

Influence that conforms to its following.
To continue this way is humiliating.

Looking to how much you can make out of a situation, or how you can influence others right now is not the way to act. Your mind isn't clear, and clarity is called for. You must reassess.

Line 4

Persevere in the good. Remorse will pass.
If one strains, few will follow.

Keep to your course. Listen to your inner self and follow the voice you hear. Don't try to manipulate situations or other people. Remember clarity of mind is paramount.

Line 5

> Influence with a firm will: no confusion.
> Influence with a stiff neck: no effect.

You are determined and steadfast. You will not be swayed. Try to be less rigid. Bend a little. Other people will respect your flexibility.

Line 6

> The influence of a wagging tongue.

When it comes to stating your case, you are strong. However, you are sometimes weak when it comes to following through. Avoid idle gossip, and learn that to make your mark it is not enough to talk; you must also act, and do so in the correct manner.

(32) Heng – Persistence

Other keywords: Duration/unchanging/marriage/continuity.

Component trigrams: Wind below, Thunder above.

Modern meaning: Stick to your course. Traditional methods are best right now. Rash behaviour would be wrong. Listen to others.

Interpretation

Learning from the past and continuing into the present are the meanings behind this hexagram. Partnerships are strongly favoured.

Judgement

> Duration is continuity in change.
> Duration succeeds through self-renewal.

Things change and alter. We must also. We must, however, remember to have an enduring meaning to our lives.

Image

> As thunder and wind: mobile yet enduring:
> Thus does the wise man stand firm.

Don't change direction. Be prepared to wait should circumstances demand it. Remember it is necessary to adapt to new situations and new trends.

Line meanings

Line 1

> Seeking duration too hastily, one fails.
> To want too much immediately is wrong.

You have acted rashly and thus changed your course. Don't take on too much as you will fail. You have lost your continuity somewhere.

Line 2

> As inner strength comes, remorse goes.

Be realistic in your aims. Don't aim so high that it becomes improbable that you can reach your goal. Listen to your inner voice a little more.

Line 3

> Without duration in one's character,
> Disgrace and persistent humiliation.

Don't let other people's fears get to you. You have had some embarrassing situations lately and have let them affect you. These have happened because of the way you have acted. Learn from these things. It is part of the learning process, and life is all about continuing to learn and to grow.

LINE 4

Duration in character is not enough.
Persistence in search is not enough.

If you keep looking for things which aren't there, you are bound to fail. To solve your problems it is necessary to look at them clearly and face up to facts. Don't make any decisions unless it is in the cold light of day. Remember that things often look very different at night.

LINE 5

Duration acquired through following
Brings good fortune to a wife
But misfortune to a husband

Be flexible and adaptable. Stick to tradition by all means, but learn to adapt it at times. Don't try to be something you aren't. This line concerns any partnerships or allegiances. Be true to yourself.

LINE 6

Enduring restlessness is harmful.

Try to take your time and stop chasing your tail. You will never reach your goal if you are forever in a hurry. This is only making you restless, and you end up with delays. Calm down and take your time. 'Patience', as they say, 'is a virtue'. Learn to acquire it! Remember the story of the hare and the tortoise; steady progress is better than bursts of frantic activity.

(33) Tun — Withdrawal

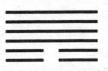

Other keywords: Retreat.

Component trigrams: Mountain below, Heaven above.

Modern meaning: Difficult situations lie ahead. You may need to withdraw, but at the right time and not before. Be practical.

Interpretation

Retreat does not mean giving up. It is wise to withdraw a little at times in order to see the situation in perspective. It is also sometimes necessary to withdraw negative emotions, as they serve no useful purpose.

Judgement

> Seek success only in small matters.
> Persevere thus, in accord with the time.

Act when the time is right to do so, not before, and not after. To act too quickly would bring loss of power and prestige. To act too late would bring further conflict. Timing is all important.

Image

> As heaven retreats before the mountain,
> Thus does the wise man keep his distance.

Looking inward to one's inner thoughts and actions is often a wise choice. It shows strength of character and dignity.

Line meanings

Line 1

>At the tail end of retreat: Danger.
>Keep still. Don't even wish to act.

If you are at the back of a battalion, you are more open to attack. Basically you haven't given yourself sufficient time to withdraw and it is better, in the current circumstances, for you to stay still. Don't act. Be careful of what you do and say, as others are waiting for you to make a mistake.

Line 2

>Hold fast to the right by force of will.
>Then none can tear one loose.

You need to be strong, correct in manner and purpose in order to win through. Someone may be able to help you. They may be stronger than you, and you should accept their help.

Line 3

>A halted retreat is nerve-racking.
>Retain only those who cling to one:
>A good act. But not for great ends.

Other people are holding you back. This is dangerous. Try to explain your need to withdraw for the moment, and enlist their aid. If they can't understand, try to retreat on your own.

Line 4

>Voluntary retreat brings favour,
>But, to the small man, downfall.

You think that retreat is the same as capitulation: it isn't. You are doing the wisest thing. Don't feel guilty. You must back off a little at this time.

Line 5

> Friendly retreat. Persevere, firm in will.
> Do not be led astray by side issues.

Keep to your chosen course. Don't let other people or other things detract from your goal. Other people will now understand you.

Line 6

> Cheerful retreat. One has no doubts.

Sometimes things don't go the way we would wish, and we must either go backwards or put aside our wishes for the time being. This is what is happening now. Accept it with a cheerful attitude, for it is fate.

(34) Ta Chuang – The Power of Greatness

Other keywords: Great strength.

Component trigrams: Heaven below, Thunder above.

Modern meaning: Be sure to follow through on anything you say. This is a fortunate time. Act wisely.

Interpretation

Things are going well and look promising. Don't take advantage of this period by overstepping yourself. Other people will be looking to you at this time. Be sure you give a good example.

JUDGEMENT

> Strength in movement: the basis of power.
> Greatness is nothing without rightness.

Don't get carried away with yourself. Acting in haste now would not be a good thing. Be firm and strong and realise it is sometimes necessary to take a break, both for your own good and that of your projects.

IMAGE

> As thunder moves in accord with heaven,
> So too, the wise man accords with the right.

Don't get sidetracked, or allow yourself to fall into bad company. It is important now to be seen to be beyond reproach.

LINE MEANINGS

LINE 1

> Advancing by force brings misfortune.

Don't act out of a sense of desperation. Pushing the pace now would bring failure.

LINE 2

> The gates to success begin to open.
> Perseverance brings good fortune.

Things are starting to look good for you. Stick with it and don't give up. Don't get too carried away, as there's still some way to go yet.

LINE 3

> The small man works through power;
> The wise man does not act this way.
> A goat that butts against a hedge
> Only gets its horns entangled.

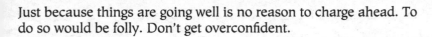

Just because things are going well is no reason to charge ahead. To do so would be folly. Don't get overconfident.

Line 4

> Persevere. Success comes: remorse goes.
> The hedge opens: no entanglement.
> A big cart's power lies in its axle.

Make sure you follow through with what you intend to do. Your strength lies with the foundations you put down right now. Don't be too hasty: think things through carefully.

Line 5

> One loses one's goat. Good. No regret.

Goats are well known to be stubborn and difficult. The goat represents you. You have now decided to do something about these negative qualities, which is a good thing. Make sure you are tolerant.

Line 6

> A goat butts a hedge and gets entangled.
> It can neither go forward nor backward.
> Take note: thus to overcome one's mistake.

Sometimes when you push too hard and too far, you reach a stalemate. This is the danger now. Make sure you are careful. If you feel this has already happened, the only way out is to back down.

(35) Chin — Advancement

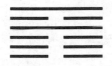

Other keywords: Progress.

Component trigrams: Earth below, Fire above.

Modern meaning: Chances for promotion or advancement are now around you. Honesty is the best policy for you. Think of others.

Interpretation

This hexagram concerns the chance to progress. It also concerns the need to balance out positive and negative. You may be able to do this by forming a union with another person who has some of the qualities you lack.

Judgement

> A devoted prince brings others with him
> To pledge fealty and peace to his king.
> He is given honour, reward and influence.

For a person to exert any influence, he must be a good leader but also command respect by wishing to help those in his team. This way, nobody is likely to be jealous, as his honesty will shine through.

Image

> As the sun rises over the earth,
> Thus does the wise man brighten his virtue.
> In 'Devotion to Great Clarity' is a path.

People are born innocent and free of evil. If they walk in the light, they remain so. Those who become wrapped up in materialism are likely to stray from the path.

Line meanings

Line 1

> Progressing but turned back. Persevere.

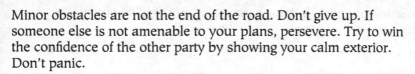

Minor obstacles are not the end of the road. Don't give up. If someone else is not amenable to your plans, persevere. Try to win the confidence of the other party by showing your calm exterior. Don't panic.

Line 2

> Progressing but frustrated. Persevere.

You feel you are blocked in getting the help you want from the person you feel is there to help you. Don't give up even if you feel like doing so. Maybe you should adopt a different tactic.

Line 3

> Progressing together. Remorse vanishes.

Sharing things with others brings great rewards. There is nothing wrong with relinquishing your independence at this time.

Line 4

> Progressing like a rat brings danger.

Legge's translation refers to a groundhog. Such animals scurry about, seeking to remain inconspicuous. Maybe that's how you are acting. Is this really wise? Be careful.

Line 5

> Take not gain and loss to heart;
> What matters is one's blessing.

You can't win every battle, and there is a sense of regret that you aren't more successful and more influential. What really matters is what you are, not who you are. Other people may be working with you now. Stick with them, even though you may think you are losing sight of your goal.

Line 6

> Progress by force. Beware of dangers.

Don't force the pace too much, but do make sure you act positively.

Keep to your path, but don't push too hard, and be sure not to fragment your energies.

(36) Ming I – Darkening of the Light

Other keywords: Fading light.

Component trigrams: Fire below, Earth above.

Modern meaning: Don't let yourself become too downhearted. Things will soon get better. Make a few plans. Don't change course.

Interpretation

This hexagram is the total opposite to the previous one. Things aren't going well, and it is easy to become depressed, but you should try to hide your true feelings, as others will become easily bored with someone moaning all the time. Don't give in to the situation, or to other people.

Judgement

> In adversity one must be persevering.
> The light is veiled, not extinguished.
> By clarity within and devotion without
> One can overcome the greatest adversity.

Remaining calm irrespective of what is going on around you makes for a wise person. Perseverance will pay off in the end.

Image

> As the light sinks into the earth,
> So does the wise man live with the world:
> He veils his light, yet still he shines.

Exercising caution is the best course of action now. In your interactions with others, make sure you don't come across as boastful or full of self-importance.

Line meanings

Line 1

> Flight and deprivation, but one has a goal.

Legge's translation refers to a man leaving home, not eating for three days and being scorned. This line suggests that evading the issue and trying to sweep a problem under the carpet will bring about greater problems in the future. There may be a lot of unwarranted gossip about you, and even close friends may wonder about your motives. It is best to withdraw at the moment.

Line 2

> Though wounded, one can still give aid.

Things can be turned round. Other people may be able to help, if you let them. Likewise, you may be able to offer help to them, should you choose to do so.

Line 3

> The dark one is captured. Avoid haste.

If you have the opportunity to put right some wrongs, do so. Don't just seek to avoid the situation. You may have upset someone, and they have every right to react towards you with hostility.

LINE 4

> One gets to the heart of the darkness;
> One must leave to save oneself.

You are in a difficult situation but should remain calm. Back off.

LINE 5

> If one cannot leave one's post,
> Persevere with redoubled caution.

Legge's translation refers to the dark times of Prince Chi. This person was the Chinese equivalent of Hamlet, who pretended to be mad. However, unlike Hamlet, Chi did nothing other than avoiding conflict. This line suggests that to protect yourself it may be best to conceal your true emotions, yet remain true to your path.

LINE 6

> The dark power reaches its climax;
> Then it perishes of its own darkness.

You have been patient and times are now turning for the better. Nothing evil lasts. The darkness is making way for the light.

(37) Chia Jen – Family

Other keywords: Clan.

Component trigrams: Fire below, Wind above.

Modern meaning: Family life is under the spotlight. An exercising of authority will be necessary. Be fair and tolerant. The women of the house should perhaps make any decisions.

INTERPRETATION

This hexagram concerns everything to do with family life, with the foundation of the husband and wife. It concerns ethical and moral codes and ways of behaving. It also concerns love and respect.

JUDGEMENT

A good wife is persevering and loyal.

The woman of the household often shoulders the most responsibility, especially when bringing up the children and teaching modes of behaviour. She also supports her husband, with whom she shares a common bond.

IMAGE

As wind comes forth from fire,
So the wise man's words have substance,
For he has duration in his way of life.

Consistency in words and action are necessary to bring about the best effects. Don't say one thing and yet do another. This will bring about failure. Make sure you practise what you preach.

LINE MEANINGS

LINE 1

A child in firm seclusion. No regrets.

It is necessary to set rules and regulations in order for everyone to know where they stand. This line suggests that it is necessary to accept the responsibilities we have, and make firm foundations for the future, so that 'the child', which may be a project or a relationship, may grow up properly.

LINE 2

The wife should not follow her whims.

Don't try to take on anything new right now. You have enough to do without adding to it. The temptations may be strong, but you will only end up chasing your tail.

LINE 3

When tempers flare and one is too severe:
Remorse. Good fortune, none the less,
For to dally all day ends in disgrace.

Don't be too severe with yourself or with others. Neither, however, should you choose the option which promises more freedom. It is best to have a certain amount of freedom within set parameters, and it would be more useful now to concentrate on such things rather than on others which promise greater success.

LINE 4

The wife is the treasure of the house.

You are being very fair-minded and unselfish. You cherish those close to you, and they feel this. Everything is well balanced. This is how it should be.

LINE 5

As a king, should he govern his family.

You know your capabilities and are sure of yourself. This makes you happy and you treat others with respect and love.

LINE 6

The master's work commands respect.

As you increase in power and authority, your character must alter to accommodate the change. You should try to be strong, consistent and fair and provide a stability for yourself and those around you. Remain true to yourself at all costs, as this is vital to growth.

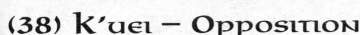

(38) K'uei – Opposition

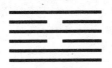

Other keywords: Neutrality/division.

Component trigrams: Marsh below, Fire above.

Modern meaning: As with yin and yang, opposites can also be complementary. Try to achieve this balance in your life. Anything inharmonious needs to be changed. Small projects will meet the greater success.

Interpretation

This hexagram is all about interaction between opposite forces. It involves situations of opposing opinions, conflict and stagnation. It also concerns the feeling of being pulled in two differing directions.

Judgement

> Opposition in small matters leads to union
> And thence to good fortune.
> Great indeed is the effect
> Of the time of opposition.

Don't act too quickly when things aren't going your way. To do so would be folly. Make headway in small steps. Unity will follow.

Image

> As fire and water never commingle
> And, even in contact, retain their natures;
> So, amid all fellowship,
> The wise man retains his individuality.

If one is truly wise, one is not led by others into things which go against the grain. Remaining an individual is what life is all about.

Line meanings

Line 1

> If you lose your horse, do not chase it.
> It will come back of its own accord.
> If you see evil people, avoid mistakes.

Something is missing in your life. Don't worry, as this is part of growing. Be amenable to new ideas. If you chase after things that you feel are lost, you will chase them further away. This applies equally to people who are no longer part of your life. Try to avoid people who have no principles. You can't change them.

Line 2

> One meets his lord in a narrow street.

Meeting someone by accident, things will change for you. It is possible that this may be a person you were seeking to avoid for some reason. It will be good that you have met. Things will be better.

Line 3

> One sees oneself hindered and insulted.
> Not a good beginning, but a good end.

You feel frustrated by blockages in your path. Nothing seems to be going well for you. Things will change in due time for the better and balance the situation. Sticking with things and people you know is better right now than treading an unknown path.

Line 4

> Isolated through opposition. Danger.
> One meets a like-minded companion.
> Association in good faith. No blame.

You meet someone who is like you and is going through the same problems. You feel less isolated, and more able to cope.

Line 5

> A companion overcomes the estrangement.
> One should go with him and find blessing.

You are happy in your companionship and friendship with someone. You don't feel so isolated. The person you have as a friend is sincere and honest. You are lucky.

Line 6

> One sees one's friends as sly. Danger.
> Then tension goes and union comes.

Don't think things of those around you which are unjustified. It just serves to create tensions. They are sincere, and if you treat them in like manner, all problems between you will go.

(39) Chien — Halting

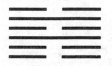

Other keywords: Difficulty/obstruction.

Component trigrams: Mountain below, Water above.

Modern meaning: Solve your problem and don't moan. Others may help. Think about it before acting. A hard time lies ahead.

Interpretation

The difficulties you are facing are necessary as part of the process of growth. They are fate, and you can do nothing about them other than learn to accept them, quietly and calmly.

JUDGEMENT

To see danger and know how to stand still;
That is wisdom.
One should pause and seek wise counsel.

Other people may be able to help you. You should think long and hard before acting, and possibly enter into a meditation to seek the wisdom to deal with the situation in a proper fashion.

IMAGE

Water on a mountain: progress obstructed.
Thus a wise man turns inward to himself;
Thus does he mould his character.

Raising the level of your own consciousness often helps you to see problems in a new light and clarity.

LINE MEANINGS

LINE 1

When going ahead leads to obstructions,
One should retreat and wait.

Pushing ahead regardless would lead to further problems. Sit back and wait.

LINE 2

A king's servant, beset by obstructions.
If one's path of duty leads to danger,
Then one must confront it. No blame.

As it is necessary for you to confront your problems, then you must do so.

Line 3

A father is obstructed, so he comes back.

You would be wrong to push ahead right now because you have responsibilities to others who would be affected by this action. Back off. Think about the problem, what has brought it about and what you can do about it. Remember that inaction now will lead to renewed strength for the action yet to come.

Line 4

When going leads to obstructions,
Coming back leads to union with friends.

Other people can help you if you ask them. They won't offer help in case their help is rejected. It is up to you to ask, having explained yourself fully to them. You can't do everything on your own, even if you think you can.

Line 5

The greatest obstructions bring help.

You have helped someone else and got into difficulties. However, you will win through because you undertook to help in good faith. Others will see that you only have the best intentions, and will offer support.

Line 6

It furthers one to see the great man.

The wise man has withdrawn from the world and its problems. Sometimes this is how you feel. However, life isn't like that, and you can't. The period of reflection you have had should help you see things more clearly. You can't just ignore problems and hope they will go away of their own accord, much as you would like that to be the case. The only possible path to success now is to be realistic and face problems head on.

Note Hexagram 53 also has the same Chinese name, but is totally different in form and meaning.

(40) Chieh — Removing Obstacles

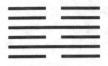

Other keywords: Release/deliverance.

Component trigrams: Water below, Thunder above.

Modern meaning: Act, but not too quickly. Solve the problem and return to your path. Don't dwell on what went wrong.

Interpretation

Things are just about to turn for the better. Put the past behind you, remembering the lessons learnt, but not bringing the past forward into the present by dwelling on it all the time. You should try not to get carried away with the prospect of a brighter future, for it is not yet here.

Judgement

> At the time of deliverance
> One should seek to return to the regular.
> If there are things to be done,
> One should attend to them quickly.

Tensions are running high. You need to get back to order. Get on with it and this will happen. However, it would be dangerous to push too far or too hard. Go back to your path.

Image

> As thunder and rain deliver nature,
> So does the wise man pardon and forgive.

Clearing the air is necessary to clear the tensions and stresses. Mental clarity is also necessary. With a clear head, you can move forward.

Line meanings

Line 1

> When deliverance has come,
> Take rest, keep still and use few words.

You can take a rest from your troubles. Sit down, relax in the quiet and gather your strength.

Line 2

> He catches cunning foxes in the field
> And receives a yellow arrow as reward.
> By perseverance comes inner strength.

You are not yet out of the woods, and should beware of those people who seek to trick you because they see good fortune coming your way. Your energies are still low. Take care.

Line 3

> A peasant rides in a golden carriage.
> To persist this way leads to disgrace.

Be careful of those around you. Don't make it clear that good fortune is now yours. There are some in your circle of friends who are not what they seem. Deceit is all around you. Take care.

Line 4

> Deliver yourself from inferior people.
> Only then can come trustworthy friends.

Look at your circle of friends. Those who are merely hangers-on should be removed. They are not true friends but acquaintances. If you fail to do this, those real friends you have may choose to leave. It is up to you now. Nobody else can do this for you.

LiNE 5

> The wise man must deliver himself
> And so to prove, to the small, his resolve.

Things are moving in the right direction, and it is necessary for you to continue the weeding out of those who no longer have a place within your circle. Likewise, you must weed out those parts of yourself which no longer have a place, and begin enlightenment.

LiNE 6

> A wise man bides his time, then acts.
> Deliverance by force is a last resort.

When there is no alternative but to use force, this must be done. Meditate upon your problem and seek spiritual guidance from within.

Note Hexagrams 40 and 60 have the same Chinese name.

(41) SuN – DecReAse

Other keywords: Reducing

Component trigrams: Marsh below, Mountain above.

Modern meaning: Watch your spending, and share things with others. You may be called upon to make a small sacrifice in one area of your life. Do so without reluctance, as you will ultimately benefit. Avoid any kind of excesses.

INTERPRETATION

A slight setback is indicated by this hexagram. It is all about a loss of some kind. Remember what comes round, goes round, and all will be well in the end.

JUDGEMENT

> At a time of decrease,
> Sincerity brings great good fortune. No blame.
> God accepts the simplest sacrifice.

Losses need not necessarily be bad. Sometimes it is necessary to have a loss to understand the gains. Times when it is necessary to watch our spending and avoid excesses teach us something.

IMAGE

> As a lake below enriches a mountain above;
> As decrease below gives increase above;
> Thus does the wise man curb his passions.

Going overboard with passions and excesses leads to problems. It is often necessary to impose restrictions on yourself. Now is that time.

LINE MEANINGS

LINE 1

> Self-decrease to serve others is good.
> How much may one decrease others?

Use your time to help other people. Just because your way is blocked is no reason to sit back. Other people could do with a hand, provided your wish to help is genuine and not just a means of self-engrandisement. Should you be the person in need of help, don't make unnecessary demands on others.

LINE 2

Increasing others
Without decreasing oneself.

Only do something with which you feel comfortable. Don't do something which is against your principles. Be true to yourself and don't lose your own dignity.

LINE 3

Increase and decrease: both give measure.
Two is company; three is too many.
One man alone needs a companion.

There is one too many in your group, and jealousies and resentment have arisen. It is necessary to reduce the numbers. It may be that you are the person who needs to go. If this is so, find someone else to go with you, as it is best that you have a companion.

LINE 4

By decreasing one's faults and one's self
One increases one's circle. No mistake.

If someone offers to help you, let them, as they need to feel they can contribute something to your cause. Others may feel that they can't help, even though they would like to. Accept help when it is offered. Being stubborn does not pay dividends.

LINE 5

One is increased, indeed, by blessing.

A period of good luck. Fate smiles on you, and you can do no wrong.

Line 6

> If one is increased, no blame. Persevere.
> Seek not private gain, but helpers.

If you keep going, and are sincere and just, you will succeed. Others will offer to help you, as they see your motives are honest. Friendships will flourish.

Note   Hexagrams 41 and 57 have the same Chinese name.

(42) I — Increase

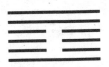

Component trigrams: Thunder below, Wind above.

Modern meaning: Luck is with you and you can go ahead with your plans. You can do no wrong; even when you make mistakes things turn out well.

Interpretation

Everything is going well. There may be a journey over water, as water is featured in the meanings of this hexagram. Others will help you without strings. A good time.

Judgement

> As the moon waxes, but then wanes;
> As do the seasons come and go;
> So the time of increase does not endure.
> We should utilise it, whilst it lasts,
> To undertake something great.

Make the most of good times. When you take the time to help others less fortunate, you will reap rewards.

Image

> As thunder and wind reinforce each other,
> So the wise man notes the ways of others.
> If he sees good in others, he imitates it;
> If he sees bad in himself, he removes it.

This is all about self-improvement and self-awareness. Sometimes it is necessary to weed out the bad parts of our make-up and build on the good parts, having seen and appreciated these qualities in others.

Line meanings

Line 1

> One should undertake something great.
> Good fortune comes from selflessness.

If you want to tackle something big, now is the time to do so, irrespective of what it is. You are full of energy right now. If others wish to help, let them, as their motives are unselfish.

Line 2

> Love of the good brings real increase.

Everything is in balance, and you can do no wrong. Good luck surrounds you. Don't get carried away, however, with all this good fortune. Keep to your path.

Line 3

> One is enriched, even by misfortune,
> If one is sincere and correct.

You have the opportunity to help someone else who is less fortunate than you. Do so, and you may even get a pat on the back!

Line 4

> He who reports to the prince
> Must walk in the middle.

The chance to mediate comes before you. You are trusted and your opinion is valued. It is good that this responsibility is being placed on your shoulders. Help as much as you can.

Line 5

> True kindness does not seek honours:
> It acts from inner necessity.

Recognition for good works comes to you.

Line 6

> He, who increases no one, brings misfortune.

If you are cold and distant, you will have no friends, even if you are generous in other ways. Open up and try to be generous in all aspects of your life, and that includes being generous with your time on behalf of other people.

Note Hexagrams 42 and 27 have the same Chinese name.

(43) Kuai — Breakthrough

Other keywords: Resoluteness/overflow.

Component trigrams: Heaven below, Marsh above.

Modern meaning: Losses are possible and you must take precautions to minimise them. Be firm but not pushy. Friendships should be cultivated.

INTERPRETATION

It is stupid to assume that everyone will always agree with you and that everything will always turn out for the best. Talking things through with friends is a good idea. Enlist the aid of others if you can.

JUDGEMENT

> By resolution is evil overcome;
> In high places, denounced despite danger;
> In oneself, not by force but by the good.

Be strong, steadfast and honest. Don't use direct force. Stick to the path. Sometimes in life it is necessary to be resolute; now is one of those times.

IMAGE

> As water rises to heaven to give rain;
> So the wise man dispenses his riches.

There is a difference between firmness and being downright stubborn. Remember, pride comes before a fall. Be aware of your own shortcomings and seek to redress any shortfall.

LINE MEANINGS

LINE 1

To over-reach oneself is a mistake.

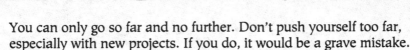

You can only go so far and no further. Don't push yourself too far, especially with new projects. If you do, it would be a grave mistake.

Line 2

> Despite danger and alarm, fear nothing.
> One is forearmed with caution.

Be on your guard for the unforeseen, and you need not be afraid. Anticipation of problems is half the battle.

Line 3

> Despite censure and gossip, be resolved.
> Remain true to yourself. No blame.

There are times when you feel everything and everyone is against you. You feel the target of gossip and feel misunderstood. Remain calm and stick to your principles, even when you feel people are turning against you.

Line 4

> Inner obstinacy. Good counsel ignored.

This is not the time to push forward. Listen to any advice offered. Don't be so pig-headed and obstinate. Back off.

Line 5

> Dealing with weeds requires resolution.

It is impossible to rid the world of evil, in the same way as it is impossible to rid the world of weeds. You must learn to live with the situation as it exists. The only true way is to cultivate the good. The evil will then fall a poor second.

Line 6

> A seeming victory. Then misfortune.

Don't become careless just because you sense the end of the bad times. It would be dangerous to do so. When you think you have won a battle, that is the most difficult time of all. Remember this.

(44) Kou – Meeting

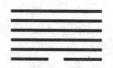

Other keywords: Temptation/encountering.

Component trigrams: Wind below, Heaven above.

Modern meaning: Stand your own ground and don't waver. Following someone else's path would be wrong. Don't enter into any contracts right now.

Interpretation

This hexagram is all about dangerous situations and unfavourable events. It is also about learning from these things for the future, and accepting losses as part and parcel of growth.

Judgement

> The way of the inferior men increases
> Because superior men lend them power.

The only way the weak rise to the top is through tricking the powerful into believing that they are harmless. In this way the powerful are seduced by the weak.

Image

> As the wind encounters all under heaven,
> So the wise ruler spreads his commands.

It is not always necessary to be in a hands-on situation to be involved. It is just as easy to command respect and be in charge as it is to get totally involved.

LINE MEANINGS

LINE 1

Even a lean pig has it in him to rage.

Keep to your path, even if you think things are against you. Like the lean pig seeking food, you are difficult to hold back now.

LINE 2

In penning the pig; be gentle; be firm.

You may feel frustrated and unable to advance, but you have brought this on yourself. Keep your frustrations within. Giving vent to them now would bring problems.

LINE 3

Temptation and painful indecision.
Aware of danger, one avoids big mistakes.

Don't give in to things which you feel are wrong. Forewarned is forearmed. Remain calm.

LINE 4

Aloof because ambitious. Misfortune.

Don't allow yourself to become detached from others who have less than you have. Remain in touch with the common people, even if you are now in a position of power. Your position has separated you from others. Should you now fall from grace, you would have no friends.

LINE 5

As a ripe fruit falls from heaven,
So others fall to one's disposition.

If you are true, honest, sincere and genuine, fate will deal you good cards with which to play. Think of others as well as yourself. Be true to yourself. There is no need to go round impressing others.

LINE 6

> If the high and proud wish to be so
> Then one should let them be.

You have done what you thought was best and have now withdrawn. Others may not understand this. As a result, you may feel hated and despised. Does this really matter? You know you did what you had to do, and it shouldn't matter too much that other people can't see this. You have been true to yourself. Let others get on with their lives; the feelings they have will eventually create problems for them.

(45) Ts'ui – Gathering Together

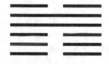

Other keywords: Accord/assembling.

Component trigrams: Earth below, Marsh above.

Modern meaning: To create harmony in your relationships, be sincere and open. Think before you speak. If you feel alone in a project seek one helper only. A hard time may lie ahead.

INTERPRETATION

This hexagram is all about gathering with others for a harmonious balance to exist. It concerns happiness with inner calm. Be prepared for a period during which this calmness will be put to the test.

Judgement

> When the king approaches the temple,
> One should come too, with one's offering,
> For this is a time of great undertakings.

The religious significance here is compounded by the fact that the leader is present. To be effective as a leader, the king must be strong and inwardly calm. He is then able to defend his people. The judgement suggests you must be likewise.

Image

> As a lake gathers the waters on earth,
> So also, men come to gather together.
> Then does the wise man renew his weapons,
> In order to meet the unforeseen.

It is necessary to take precautionary measures, as a large group is an obvious target. Be prepared for unexpected events.

Line meanings

Line 1

> Without a leader, wills grow confused:
> One who can lead brings laughter.

The person who is considered leader of any group must be the strongest and have the strongest principles. There is someone like that around you to whom you can turn with your problems. Do so, and you won't go far wrong.

Line 2

> Letting oneself be drawn by affinity:
> Even one's small offering is acceptable.

If you feel that you are drawn to a person or to a group, don't be afraid and go with your feelings. Listen to your inner voice and be guided by it.

LiNe 3

> If one is an outsider, seek alliance:
> In spite of humiliation, this way is right.

You feel isolated from a group of other people. You would like to be part of that group, and are wondering whether you should try to join in. Do so. If you never ask, you will never be part of the group. They are waiting for you to say that you are interested in joining them.

LiNe 4

> A minister who gathers men around him,
> In the name of his ruler, brings favour.

Working for other people without reward is the message here. Legge's translation merely states that accord is approaching. Things are going in the right direction.

LiNe 5

> A leader gains sway. No blame in this.
> He must also win the insincere.

If you are in charge of a group of people, it is necessary to win their trust. If you are part of a group, it is necessary to be honest with the others about any anxieties you have. Communication is the key here on both sides. Make your feelings clear, whether you are leader or follower.

LiNe 6

> Lamenting and sighing, floods of tears:
> This is the right way. It may succeed.

Sometimes other people fail to understand your motives and this causes you concern. Don't worry, because eventually the others will understand and a good bond will be created between you. It is good to show your feelings. This is part of being true to yourself. It also helps other people understand what really makes you tick.

(46) Sheng – Ascending

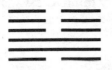

Other keywords: Pushing upward/rising.

Component trigrams: Wind below, Earth above.

Modern meaning: Progress may be slow, but go forwards with your plans. Consulting a professional person could help solve a problem. A good time.

Interpretation

This hexagram, comprising the trigrams for earth and wood (also called wind), immediately gives the idea of a tree growing from the soil, forever upwards. Likewise, this hexagram is all about growth from small beginnings. Like the tree, the development may take time, but will be well worth it.

Judgement

> Pushing upward has supreme success.
> One should see great men: seek advice:
> Set to work for activity is favoured.

Nothing is standing as a barrier in your path to advancement. Other people may be able to help and you should get to work. The signs are good.

Image

> As wood grows within the earth,
> So the wise man of devoted character,

> Heaps up small things
> To achieve something high and great.

From small beginnings, big things are achieved. The tree doesn't pause in its growth, but keeps going. So must you.

Line meanings

Line 1

> Pushing upward meets with confidence.
> Thus can something be accomplished.

You feel you have only one foot on the ladder of success, and the ladder seems so very tall. Remember everything starts from humble beginnings. Even the tree starts as a small shoot. Don't give up.

Line 2

> If one is sincere and upright
> One should bring even a small offering.

It seems you still have a long way to go to achieve your aims. However, your sincerity shines through, and others who see your struggle will look kindly upon you.

Line 3

> Easy unobstructed progress.

There seems to be nothing in your path. Is this because you have opted for the easier route? Remember, things might not always be this easy.

Line 4

> The king offers one great honour.
> This is the way of the devoted.

This line suggests a promotion. The boss has seen how hard you work and feels it is right to give you a little more responsibility. If

you are not yet working, this is also a promising sign because offers are likely. Those workers for charitable or spiritual causes are likely to find themselves highly regarded for their sincerity and devotion.

LINE 5

> Pushing upward by steps. Persevere.

Don't get carried away by how well things are going. You are so near to your goal now that it would be easy to become over-confident. You aren't there yet. Keep to your path and continue to work at it. Take your time and don't try any shortcuts.

LINE 6

> Pushing upwards in darkness. Exhaustion.
> One must persevere unremittingly.

Your ambitions know no barriers. You are blind to the realities of situations. This leads to failure. You need to know where you are aiming for to be able to reach it, and to be able to realise when you have reached it. Working hard with sincerity is the only way. Don't look back, but remember your aims and stick to them.

(47) K'UN — REPRESSION

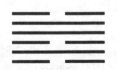

Other keywords: Oppression/exhaustion/contraction.

Component trigrams: Water below, Marsh above.

Modern meaning: Things are looking hard, but maintain your composure, and keep silent where possible. Dig deep within yourself to find the strength to cope. You will if you are determined enough.

INTERPRETATION

This hexagram concerns barren and unfruitful times when you must seek your own inner strength, and not be panicked into doing things which you may later regret. It is a time when material things may be lost. If this happens, it is necessary to realise that they may not have been essentials – merely trappings which you could do without.

JUDGEMENT

> Oppression is a test of character:
> It leads to perplexity and thence to success.
> When one has something to say
> One gets no hearing; one is not believed.
> But through oppression does one learn
> To lessen one's rancour.

Even hard times can produce benefits, if you learn from the pitfalls you experience and remain outwardly cheerful about it all. It is ultimately how you act and not what you say which makes you wise.

IMAGE

> The lake is dried up, exhausted.
> When adverse fate befalls him,
> The wise man stakes his life
> On following his will.

When things are going against you, it is often best to accept, realising that it is fate and that resistance is useless.

LINE MEANINGS

LINE 1

> One sits oppressed under a bare tree:
> One strays into a gloomy valley.

You have given up trying and have sunk into a depression. This has made things seem even worse than they are. Try to snap out of it.

LINE 2

> Oppressed whilst at meat and drink.

You have everything you want, but are offered the chance of more. It is necessary to think about the offer.

LINE 3

> One feels oppressed by walls of stone:
> One leans on thorns and thistles.

You want to push ahead, but seem forever to meet with obstacles. This is probably because you are going about things in the wrong way, or are making problems for yourself. Reassess your actions. Talk it through with the family.

LINE 4

> Oppressed whilst in a golden carriage.

Other people in a less powerful position than you may be able to help if you let them. Maybe you feel you are better than them, and this is making you feel guilty. The only difference between you is your success.

LINE 5

> Oppressed with good intentions.

It takes time for things to improve. Don't be so impatient. Bide your time wisely.

LINE 6

> Oppressed by bonds one can now break.

You need to make a move but feel you can't. The only thing stopping you is yourself. Get on with it.

(48) Ching — The Well

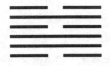

Component trigrams: Wind below, Water above.

Modern meaning: Things are good, but may still change. Be sincere, otherwise you may court disaster. You may under- or over-estimate someone or something. Be on your guard.

Interpretation

The well is the well of human nature, and learning about others as well as about yourself, normally from past experiences. There is a danger that you could get too far away from your goals at this time. Listen to your inner voice, but think things through afterwards.

Judgement

> The town may change but the well abides.
> If one's rope is too short,
> Or if one breaks the jug,
> Then one's thirst remains. Misfortune.

Things change but basic human nature remains unaltered. It is necessary to look within as well as without.

Image

> As a plant lifts water to life itself,
> So a wise ruler encourages his people
> To work and to help one another.

To run a business it is essential to create team spirit. Working with others for mutual benefit is all-important.

Line meanings

Line 1

> No one drinks the mud of the well:
> No animals come to an old well:
> Time just passes it by.

It is necessary to keep up to date. It is also necessary to remain an individual and not follow others blindly. Those who care too much can get taken for granted and lose their individuality.

Line 2

> The water is clear, but one's jug leaks.
> One has left one's well to the fishes.

You can't be bothered to get involved with other people because you feel you wouldn't be able to control the situation. You are neglecting your good qualities, and those with whom you could mix therefore want nothing to do with you.

Line 3

> The well is clear but no one drinks.
> If only the king were clear-minded,
> Good fortune could be enjoyed by all.

There is someone around who is very practical, but you aren't making use of his talents. He is upset because he needs some work to make him feel valued again. He has much to offer.

Line 4

> The well is being lined. No blame;
> Because it is being put in order.

Think of yourself first and foremost right now. You need to take time to rebuild yourself and your energies. You aren't being selfish, just taking steps to recharge your batteries. Others can fend for themselves for the time being.

LINE 5

A clear cold spring. One should drink.

Someone else is opening up to you. You may not be aware of them yet. You should seek him out, and listen to him.

LINE 6

One draws from the well. No hindrance.
It is dependable. Great blessing for all.

Learning is there for everyone. It is not limited to only a few. Spiritual learning is also there to be tapped into, should you choose to do so. Other people may well wish to learn. Be sympathetic to their wishes.

(49) Ko – Change

Other keywords: Revolution/rotation.

Component trigrams: Sun below, Marsh above.

Modern meaning: Significant change, which will concern opportunities. Smaller changes follow. Be ready, and look the part. Don't act for purely materialistic reasons.

INTERPRETATION

This hexagram concerns cyclical changes, i.e. the seasons. It also concerns social and personal changes, and changes in attitude.

Judgement

> Joyousness comes through enlightenment.
> If revolution is right, remorse will pass.
> On your own day, you are believed.
> Persevere, for thereby comes success.

Changes come, and we have to accept them. Resistance is futile. We have to further learn to bide our time and to proceed in the right way. It is often the case that we act on purely materialistic or selfish motives. We must move on from that stance now and consider other people.

Image

> As the seasons bring their revolutions,
> So the wise man makes clear their times,
> And prepares himself for their demands.

We must be able to change in response to the demands made upon us. Just as the seasons must change, so must we.

Line meanings

Line 1

> Premature revolution: evil results.
> The time for action has not yet come:
> Be firm in utmost self-restraint.

You are sometimes forced to change when there is no other alternative. Don't act too hastily. Be calm, firm and controlled.

Line 2

> Revolution only when one's day comes;
> Begin now with inner preparation.
> To go to meet it, thus, is no mistake.

Be prepared for change and then the effect it has on you will be minimised.

LINE 3

> Haste or hesitation: both bring danger.
> When talk has gone around three times,
> Then may one commit oneself.

Don't be too rash or too ruthless when meeting with change. Think about things before acting and about consulting other people for their viewpoints.

LINE 4

> Revolution founded on higher truth
> Gains support, of itself. Remorse passes.

The changes around you are quite profound. You must have the right moral codes, as well as being ethically correct. If you are looking for other people to take your corner, you must be seen to be beyond reproach.

LINE 5

> The great man makes the guidelines clear.
> Thus does he win spontaneous support.

People will only trust you if you make your aims and motives clear. If you don't they are unlikely to know what is behind the changes taking place and will keep away. Make your position firm and clear.

LINE 6

> After revolution come the minor reforms.
> Be satisfied with the attainable.

When things have settled after a major change, smaller changes occur, in the same way as the ripples of a stone hitting water eventually get smaller. Stick to what you can cope with and leave the rest.

(50) Ting – The Cauldron

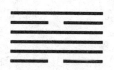

Other keywords: Sacred vessel/great bowl.

Component trigrams: Wind below, Fire above.

Modern meaning: Little things may get you down. Be prepared for problems with equipment. Things will go well for you in the main. Further success is likely. Remember to address both the material and spiritual sides of yourself.

Interpretation

The cauldron is at the centre of the house. If it is full, the home is likely to be well nourished. This hexagram is all about success, both materially and spiritually, as the cauldron was also used in temples. Harmony surrounds you.

Judgement

> The great bowl: supreme good fortune.
> Herein is the culmination of culture;
> Enlightenment and true understanding:
> Clarity comes through inner gentleness.

Again, the link between materialism and spirituality is shown. It is important to make sure both these things are equally addressed to be at one with both yourself and your God.

Image

> As fire depends on the wood within it;
> As wood within fire lends power to flame;
> Thus does a wise man give light to his life.

Living in harmony with oneself and with mankind is the true mark of a successful person. By keeping his own fire alight, he is able to show light to others.

LINE MEANINGS

LINE 1

> A Great Bowl, upturned for cleaning.
> The lowly are honoured for their works.

Look at yourself from within. Are there things about you which need cleaning or cleansing? Remember that even people who are simple in need and simple in thought can become powerful. Success can transcend barriers of class, race or gender.

LINE 2

> There is good food in one's Great Bowl.
> One is envied. Be cautious. No harm.

Other people may envy you and feel jealous about your success. This could cause problems if you allow it to do so. By remaining true to your moral and ethical code, you shouldn't be bothered too much by this.

LINE 3

> The handle is bent: one's pheasant wasted.
> One is impeded, but remorse will pass.

You are unable to share your good fortune with others, and this upsets you. Stick with it, as things will eventually change, and you will be able to do what you want.

LINE 4

> The legs of The Great Bowl are broken.
> The prince's meal is spilled
> And his person soiled. Misfortune.

There is a lot of pressure on you right now, and you feel you might snap under the strain. Be careful.

Line 5

The Great Bowl has ears of yellow.

The yellow ears are handles of gold. There are people around you who see your genuine love and humility. These people would be willing to help you, if you asked them to. Because the golden handles of the pot become hot with the fire, it cannot be lifted. Likewise you may be unable to pass on any good fortune to others. Remember to stay true to yourself.

Line 6

The Great Bowl has carrying rings of jade.

Unlike handles of gold which become hot when a bowl is used on a fire, jade handles are both precious and also useful, as they can be touched without harm. Your situation of good fortune can now be shared with others.

(51) Chen — Thunder

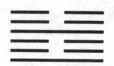

Other keywords: Thunderclap/shock/arousing.

Component trigrams: Thunder below, Thunder above.

Modern meaning: Problems ahead. Stay calm. As with a storm, it will soon pass. You may be shocked at some news. Don't let it affect you. It's probably gossip.

INTERPRETATION

Things happen suddenly and with a powerful force. It is best to ride it out and try to stay uninvolved.

JUDGEMENT

>Thunder comes, spreading terror afar;
>Shock also brings success and joy,
>For now is the time for reverence
>As God comes forth in The Arousing.

There is nothing to fear but fear itself. Learning this lesson is important for future growth.

IMAGE

>Thunder repeated: the image of shock.
>Thus, in fear and trembling,
>The wise man examines himself
>To set his life in order and to shape it.

A time to look within and put right things which need reshaping.

LINE MEANINGS

LINE 1

>Shock comes, but it leads to laughter.
>Fear brings good fortune in due course.

Don't think that you are the only person affected by current events. You are not. When you realise this, you will feel a lot happier.

LINE 2

>Shock brings danger and great losses,
>Do not go in pursuit. Withdraw.

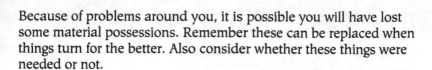

Because of problems around you, it is possible you will have lost some material possessions. Remember these can be replaced when things turn for the better. Also consider whether these things were needed or not.

Line 3

> Shock that makes one crazed with grief.
> Be spurred to inner action. No harm.

Don't let things upset you. Let fate take its course. You will be able to do something positive in due course.

Line 4

> Inner movement is mired and tough
> Because things are not clear enough.

You must be more flexible. When things are clearer, you will be able to act. Stay still now and bend a little. Be aware of opportunities as they arise, but don't go actively seeking change, as your mind isn't clear enough.

Line 5

> Shock upon shock threaten danger;
> Nothing is lost if one is correct.

There are things you must do, and providing you do things correctly, no harm will come to you. Everyone else, however, will think you are mad to do anything right now.

Line 6

> When shock brings ruin and terror,
> And one is not equal to it, keep still.

Other people are affected by problems as well as you, and to keep your sanity, it would be best if you backed off right now. Other people will be angry and volatile and it is possible there will be a lot of gossip flying around about you and others close to you. Turn a deaf ear.

(52) KEN – MOUNTAIN

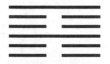

Other keywords: Keeping still/immobility.

Component trigrams: Mountain below, Mountain above.

Modern meaning: Adopt a low profile and you may avoid problems. Any risks should be avoided. Continue to work in the background for a while. This is a good time for meditation.

INTERPRETATION

This hexagram is all about keeping still. It is formed from two identical trigrams. This is a time for inner reflection.

JUDGEMENT

> Keeping one's back still
> So that restlessness dissolves;
> Beyond the tumult,
> One can perceive the great laws.

In the stillness, one often finds the thing one has been searching for; this is the time to go into the stillness.

IMAGE

> As a mountain keeps still within itself,
> Thus a wise man does not permit his will
> To stray beyond his situation.

Thoughts are living things. Now is the time to turn one's thoughts to oneself and to within.

Line meanings

Line 1

> To halt, even before beginning to move,
> Is no mistake. Be patient. Persevere.

Listen to your inner voice to guide you if you feel hesitant about a situation. Be careful and be patient.

Line 2

> One halts in time; but in sorrow,
> Because one cannot save one's master.

There are times when you can't help other people. Now is one of those times. Be true to yourself.

Line 3

> Making one's back rigid is dangerous.

Being inflexible is a big problem. Another problem lies in trying to force the pace, or force other people. Be careful.

Line 4

> To restrain oneself at the right time
> Is no mistake. It leads towards peace.

You are far more spiritually aware, but haven't reached a full state of enlightenment. When you do, you will find peace. Remember, however, you have to lose some of your ego to be truly at peace.

Line 5

> By keeping the mouth still
> One's words have order: remorse passes.

Be careful what you say. You appear to others to give little for their viewpoints. Think about what you are saying.

Line 6

> Peaceful stillness: a great blessing.

Peace, tranquillity and a calm mind are found. This is harmony and rest.

(53) Chien — Growth

Other keywords: Procession/development/gradual progress.

Component trigrams: Mountain below, Wind above.

Modern meaning: Slowly and surely should you target your progress right now. Others may think you have halted but you know otherwise. Deal with things as they crop up. Don't jump ahead.

Interpretation

Carrying on the thoughts of tranquillity and peace, this hexagram also brings in the element of staying power. Patience is a virtue which this hexagram concentrates strongly upon.

Judgement

> Development means going step by step:
> Things must follow their proper course.
> Gentleness is adaptable, yet penetrating.
> It proceeds from inner calm.

You can't rush things, especially anything involving other people. Things must go at their own pace. Likewise, to develop one's awareness and improve oneself takes time.

Image

> A mountain tree can be seen from afar:
> Thus a wise man abides, in dignity and virtue,
> In order to improve the moral order.

To be influential, one must have attained a position of authority, and be seen to be leading by example. Such things take time.

Line Meanings

Line 1

> A lonely beginning is full of danger.

As with the Fool in the Tarot deck, this is the start of a journey. It is necessary to proceed with caution, as the road is unfamiliar to you, despite past experiences. Legge's translation refers to 'talk'. Other people may wish to put forward their views. Listen to them.

Line 2

> Finding security brings reassurance
> And eating and drinking in concord.

You feel a little more secure, but things are still unsettled. Other people may want to share things with you, and it would be foolish to turn them away.

Line 3

> One goes too far. One loses one's way.

You have pushed too far too soon, and with too much aggression. You can't turn back now, and the whole situation is shaky. Be on your guard.

Line 4

> Finding a refuge amid dangers. No blame.

Strange and unexpected things have happened and you are in a difficult position as you were not prepared. You will have to put up with this and stay put for a while.

LINE 5

> One is misunderstood and misjudged;
> It leads in the end to success.

Sometimes you can turn disadvantageous situations around, and now is one of those times. Because of the speed of your success, people close to you feel upset. Some may even feel jealous and wish to see you fall. Stay with your present path, as they will soon become accustomed to the changes in your circumstances.

LINE 6

> Wild geese fly high in perfect order.

You have reached your goal, and must now prepare to find a new goal at which to aim. People look up to you. This is the start of good times and new challenges.

Note Hexagrams 53 and 39 have the same Chinese name.

(54) KUEI MEI – MARRYING MAIDEN

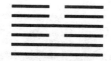

Other keywords: Young woman about to marry.

Component trigrams: Marsh below, Thunder above.

Modern meaning: You may have to alter your plans to something more attainable. Make sure what you undertake is something with which you can cope! Things will soon improve.

Interpretation

This hexagram concerns taking a subordinate role in order to win through in the end. Sometimes this is seen as backing down. To the wise, it is seen as playing the cards which have been dealt to the best advantage. It also concerns cyclic change and relationships entered into happily.

Judgement

> The marrying maiden: joyous in movement.
> Love is the basis of all true union:
> In heaven and earth, in the cycle of life,
> In the tactful reserve of a loving wife.

When a girl marries into a family, she must learn to respect their ways and not force change to suit only her needs. She must be tactful and reserved. She must remember who she is and what her role in the family has become. She is an individual within a greater unit.

Image

> As thunder stirs the surface of a lake,
> So a wise man sees transitory movement
> In the light of the eternity of the end.

In times of trouble and difficulty, when misunderstandings and setbacks occur, the sensible thing to do is remember that things will eventually settle down.

Line meanings

Line 1

> The marrying maiden: modest and tactful:
> She knows how to conduct herself.

There are times when it is best to remain in the background, and now is one of them. Even if you think you can better yourself or your position, don't do anything.

LINE 2

The girl is disappointed and lonely:
But a one-eyed man can still see.

You are in a relationship where you feel let down. Others can see this.

LINE 3

A girl just throws herself away
If she seeks to marry at any cost.

You think you want something, yet when you get it, you still aren't happy. Maybe you are looking for something which doesn't exist.

LINE 4

A good girl holds back from marriage;
Then marries the right man in due course.

Things come right in the end if you wait for them. Don't think that things have passed you by. Retain your dignity, as all will be well in the end.

LINE 5

The king gave his daughter in marriage,
But her gown was not as gorgeous
As that of the serving maid.

The person who waits often gets the best reward. Maybe you are aiming too high and should lower your sights a little. Then you may find what you are seeking.

LINE 6

She offers a basket of tainted fruit.
Empty form is empty indeed.

You can't live up to expectations. Sometimes there is nothing that you can do in such a situation. Remember, things may not be what they seem. Even something which looks good may in fact not be so brilliant after all.

(55) feng – Abundance

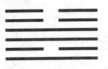

Other keywords: Prosperity/plenty/fullness.

Component trigrams: Sun below, Thunder above.

Modern meaning: Good luck and good fortune. Anything untoward will soon pass. Things are at their height now. Remember, though, that a decline may follow.

Interpretation

Power is indicated here. Also action and prosperity are shown. This hexagram is all about reaching your goal then finding new goals at which to aim which are more fulfilling.

Judgement

> The time of abundance is usually brief,
> But be not sad or sorrowing:
> Be like the sun at noon,
> Illuminating and gladdening all creation.

Things are going really well, but are still subject to change. Time and the passing of time will bring their own changes. Having achieved a materialistic goal, maybe it would be wise to address the spiritual.

Image

As thunder and lightning come together:
Inner clarity with outward action;
Thus does the wise judge decide lawsuits.
He ensures strict and precise penalties.

It is essential to have peace of mind and inner tranquillity to be truly at one with yourself. This message, mentioned in other hexagrams, is reinforced here.

Line meanings

Line 1

To work with one's destined ruler
Is no mistake, but only for so long.

You meet with someone who possesses what you lack. It could be a good partnership, as long as you remember that it will not be for ever, and are willing to sever the relationship at some point in the future.

Line 2

One sees the major stars at noon:
An eclipse looms. Mistrust and hate.

Someone has put you in the shade. This is good. Don't do anything about it. The other person will know what they have done.

Line 3

One sees even small stars at noon:
The eclipse is total. Do nothing. Wait.

You can do nothing about the situation. You will just have to wait.

Line 4

One sees the lodestar at noon:
The eclipse passes. One meets his prince.

Things are getting better. You have met the person mentioned in line one.

LINE 5

> As blessing and fame draw near for one,
> So does good fortune and blessing for all.

You are surrounded by good people. Listen to them.

LINE 6

> In his house of abundance he screens himself off.
> He peers out through the gate but no longer sees anyone.

You are unable to enjoy the fruits of your labours. You have cut yourself off from those who would wish to share in your good fortune. You have isolated yourself. There is no blame on anyone other than you.

(56) Lu — Travel

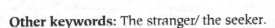

Other keywords: The stranger/ the seeker.

Component trigrams: Mountain below, Sun above.

Modern meaning: Movement or moving is indicated. Choose friends wisely. Things are changing, so avoid any long-term commitments.

INTERPRETATION

This hexagram concerns moving around and learning from that

movement. Very much like the journey of the Fool in the Tarot, this hexagram concerns both the materialistic and spiritual journey.

JUDGEMENT

The wanderer: success through smallness.
Perseverance brings him blessing.
The meaning within is truly great.

If you are good to other people, they will be good to you. Small deeds often bring large rewards.

IMAGE

As fire on the mountain tarries not;
A bright light without, yet calm within;
So the wise judge protracts no lawsuits.
In his judgements, he is clear-minded;
In imposing penalties, he is cautious.

If it is necessary to judge other people, do so quickly and without malice. Remain clear in thought and deed.

LINE MEANINGS

LINE 1

To busy oneself with trivial things
Is to miss-spend one's will. Misfortune.

There are many ways of viewing a situation. Try to be more humble and genuine. By being off-hand, you will come off the worse.

LINE 2

One comes to an inn with one's goods.
One wins a servant's steadfastness.

A wise man has a true and clear view of what and who he is. He is

able to meditate wherever he is and find calm. If he doesn't do this, he is not true to himself. Think about this.

Line 3

> One's inn burns down. Danger. Unrest.
> One loses a servant's steadfastness.

If you get involved in things which are none of your concern, you will get burned. Don't let your emotions run away with your logic. Your friends may not seem to be on your side right now. If you take your time, they will soon come round to your way of thinking.

Line 4

> One finds a shelter, with one's goods;
> Be on guard: one is not yet secure.

You may have found a temporary solution to your problems, but it is only temporary. You may have found a job for a time, but remember to look for something more permanent. You are not meant to stop there long.

Line 5

> He offers his gift. He gains recognition
> Even a stranger can find friends.

People will be nice to you, even though you are new to the job or situation. You feel more secure.

Line 6

> One lets oneself go. Joy turns to tears.

You are rash and unthinking at times. You have upset others. You have made yourself look foolish. You have been very disrespectful of other people. The damage is done, and you have to live with the consequences.

Note Hexagrams 56 and 10 have the same Chinese name.

(57) Sun – Gentle

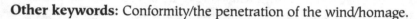

Other keywords: Conformity/the penetration of the wind/homage.

Component trigrams: Wind below, Wind above.

Modern meaning: Flexibility and going along with other people is needed right now. Someone may come to your aid. Stick to your plans but remain behind the scenes.

Interpretation

This hexagram is about being gentle in mind and action, being flexible yet getting to the heart of problems.

Judgement

> The gentle succeeds through being small.
> It furthers one to have a goal in life;
> It furthers one to see the great man.

Remaining calm and gentle, whilst having an aim in life, is the way of reaching power. Keeping on course without creating too many waves is the best path to take.

Image

> As winds follow, one upon another;
> So the wise ruler spreads his commands.

Sometimes it is necessary to seek the wisdom of others or your inner wisdom before making any moves. By so doing, others are more influenced.

Line meanings

Line 1

Irresolute drifting. No discipline.

Don't be so indecisive. Make up your mind what you want and then go for it.

Line 2

Penetration into darkest recesses:
A great effort of will finds favour.

There are things going on behind the scenes which smack of evil. Find out what these are, who is perpetrating these things and seek help from others experienced in dealing with such matters.

Line 3

Irresolute vacillation. Exhaustion.

Sometimes it is necessary to act, rather than waver. Now is such a time. If you fail to act, you will regret it.

Line 4

A man of merit: both modest and energetic.

Making sure you address all sides of your self – your material, emotional and spiritual needs – you will find yourself in a happy and contented state of mind. You will then be able to turn your attention to helping other people.

Line 5

Steadfast and careful work. Good fortune.

Things may not have been too brilliant up to now, and only you can turn them round. Think about the situation before acting. Enter into a meditation. When you have acted, think again and see what has been achieved. If you aren't satisfied, be content that you have done as much as you can right now, and leave it.

LINE 6

Penetrating the dark, one loses oneself.

The dark here refers to forces of evil. The only way to deal with this right now is to back off. You should be careful. You have to be a special kind of person to deal with such things, and you haven't got the necessary experience or strength.

Note   Hexagrams 57 and 41 have the same Chinese name.

(58) Tui — The Joyous

Other keywords: Pleasure/joy.

Component trigrams: Marsh below, Marsh above.

Modern meaning: Good news and good fortune. You are in tune with your spiritual side, and it shows. Other people will want to join forces with you. Work with them.

INTERPRETATION

You are happy, content and at peace with yourself and with others. This hexagram is about true joy and happiness.

JUDGEMENT

The joyous succeeds through steadfastness;
For if one is both joyous and steadfast,
One accords with both God and man.

You are able to show your feelings, be happy and at the same time be true to yourself. Other people will see this and know that, through hard work and effort, they too can achieve such a state of mind. People may come to you for advice. Give it.

Image

> As two lakes join to replenish each other,
> So the wise man joins with his friends
> To discuss and practise the truths of life.

Sharing knowledge and happiness makes for a joyous gathering. Helping others brings true rewards.

Line meanings

Line 1

> Contented joyousness: inner security:
> One's way is not yet hedged by doubt.

You are happy with everything around you, including those things for which you have worked. You seek nothing else. You are truly happy.

Line 2

> Sincere joyousness dispels remorse,
> If one has faith in one's will.

Don't show off when in a group of people who have less than you. Don't embarrass others by your success. Be sincere and respect those around you.

Line 3

> When joy comes from without: misfortune:
> For it causes one to lose oneself.

You seem to delight only in trivial, amusing and sensual things. You have not taken into account the spiritual side of yourself. You are in danger of losing yourself if you carry on in this way.

LINE 4

> In weighing joys, one is not at peace:
> In choosing the higher is true joy.

You are analysing things too much. This is bringing you a great deal of unhappiness. Aim for higher things, and that includes the higher spiritual elements of yourself.

LINE 5

> Disintegrating influences. Beware.

You are putting yourself in a position where you can and will be taken advantage of, so beware. Protect yourself.

LINE 6

> Seductive joyousness: he loses himself.

Pleasure is all right if it is controlled. The danger here is that you are exercising no control at all, resulting in you feeling bored with all the excesses. You seem to have lost your direction. Be careful.

(59) ḥUAN — ÓISPERSAL

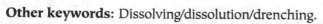

Other keywords: Dissolving/dissolution/drenching.

Component trigrams: Water below, Wind above.

Modern meaning: Find the middle road and be reasonable. Pushing too far either way would bring failure. You may meet again with people from the past, with whom you form a spiritual bond.

INTERPRETATION

This hexagram concerns coming together and also flexibility. It is possible that a journey over water will be taken.

JUDGEMENT

> Dispersion shows the way to reunion.
> The temple is the place of union.
> Union is the time for great undertakings.

Problems may be solved through the union with others with similar spiritual leanings. Co-operation with others is featured. All barriers can now come down.

IMAGE

> As the warm winds of spring stir the waters
> And dissolve even the rigidity of ice;
> So wise kings of old built temples
> To praise God; to stir and unite men.

Being isolationist leads to selfishness and hardness of heart. When people come together in love of God, they are truly united.

LINE MEANINGS

LINE 1

> Irresolute drifting. No discipline.

There are misunderstandings and confusion around you. Sort this out now. If you let things drift, they will be more difficult to resolve.

LINE 2

> When one finds oneself alienated,
> Be objective, moderate and just.

You are looking within yourself and find things you don't like. You see bigotry, bad temper, jealousy and hatred. You must do something about this. Replace these things with love, peace and sincerity.

LINE 3

> To dissolve one's self is no mistake.

You must be sure to take account of your personal needs and wishes. You are low in self-esteem, so place no importance on personal needs.

LINE 4

> Dissolving oneself from one's own party
> Brings supreme good fortune.

You should distance yourself from your friends and associates and concentrate more on matters in hand. You will also be able to see things more clearly from a distance, and realise who are true friends and who are merely hangers-on.

LINE 5

> A great idea: a rallying point.

You seem to be energetically helping other people. You have some great ideas and want to put right the wrongs of the past. This is good.

LINE 6

> Dissolving one's self to save oneself.
> To avoid danger this way is no mistake.

You are getting so carried away with things that you are in danger of going too far. A touch of realism is needed right now to bring you back from the brink.

(60) Chieh – Restraint

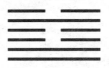

Other keywords: Regulation/limitation/restriction.

Component trigrams: Marsh below, Water above.

Modern meaning: Limitations will be placed on you. Stay calm and wait until opportunities once again come your way. Use this time to develop self-awareness.

Interpretation

This hexagram is all about limitations on growth on all fronts. It is also about using the negative and turning it to positive by being wise and forward thinking.

Judgement

> Limitation, due measure, leads to success.
> Do not persist in galling restraint,
> For its way comes to an end, to failure.

Using time wisely leads to success. If you try to change things before their time, it is unwise, in the same way as it is unwise to put limitations on self-development. It is a time to understand more about yourself, your needs, your aims and how far you can safely go.

Image

> As does a lake limit the inexhaustible;
> So does the wise man weigh and measure.
> He finds virtue in where his duty lies.

Everyone needs to know how far they can push themselves. Pushing themselves over that barrier leads to dissipation of energy and ultimately to failure.

Line meanings

Line 1

One's actions are limited. No blame.
Be discreet in limiting one's words.

Now is not the time to act. Bide your time and look within to find the answers you need. You will then know when the time is right to act.

Line 2

To limit one's action brings misfortune.

Don't miss opportunities when they come around, as they may not come around again.

Line 3

To know no limitation: cause for lament.
If one laments, one finds freedom.

You have indulged yourself with excesses. You now regret this. You are beginning to learn your limitations. Remember, the mistakes made have been yours and yours alone.

Line 4

Natural, contented limitation. Success.

You must learn to take the middle road, to compromise, both with others but more importantly with yourself. Don't push too hard. Save your energies.

Line 5

> Sweet limitation through self-limitation.
> This is the way to favour and esteem.

It is perfectly acceptable to place severe limitations on yourself, as these may be needed. You may have to put limitations on others. Don't make these too restrictive. Others need leeway.

Line 6

> Galling limitation. To persist is bad.
> Even so, one must save oneself.

You have been too restrictive with others. They resent this and may turn against you. Limit yourself a little.

Note Hexagrams 60 and 40 have the same Chinese name.

(61) Chung Fu — Inmost Sincerity

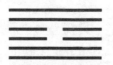

Other keywords: Understanding/inner truth.

Component trigrams: Marsh below, Wind above.

Modern meaning: Communication in the correct manner brings about favourable results. It is a good time to plan for the future.

Interpretation

You are well liked and well respected. This hexagram is all about being happy with yourself and with your life.

JUDGEMENT

> Inner truth is a forceful influence.
> It penetrates even the unhearing heart.
> Its way is through deep understanding.

It is necessary to deal with people individually, using the correct framework for them. Don't assume everyone is like everyone else. If forming a group, be aware of the need to work together, and also be aware that even the best-formed groups eventually move apart.

IMAGE

> As wind stirs water by penetration;
> Thus does the wise judge understand men.

It is necessary to understand your fellow man if you want to gain their respect.

LINE MEANINGS

LINE 1

> Inner truth comes of inner stability:
> Secret designs, of inner disquiet.

You are being underhand in your dealings. You are not treating people fairly. You are using people.

LINE 2

> Inner truth finds the responsive heart.

Legge's translation refers to a crane hearing the call of her young. This line suggests that you will feel something from within, and find it necessary to respond. This could be a spiritual awakening. Likewise, it could also indicate a stirring of emotions for someone else.

Line 3

> He finds a comrade; becomes dependent.
> Now he sobs; now he sings.

You are completely wrapped up in your relationship with someone else to the exclusion of anything and anyone else. This is unhealthy.

Line 4

> One turns oneself away to seek the light,
> As the moon turns to face the sun.

You have been rejected by someone close. You must look inwardly for help and peace.

Line 5

> In possessing truth, he holds together.

You are the focal point of your group. You manage to keep the group together. If you decide to back off now, the group will fall apart. You can't be held responsible for this. Do what you think best.

Line 6

> Cockcrowing that persists. Misfortune.

You have a gift for communication, but sometimes your mouth runs away with you. Be careful what you say. Don't exaggerate.

(62) Ḣsiao Kua – Great Smallness

Other keywords: Small excesses/small continuation.

Component trigrams: Mountain below, Thunder above.

Modern meaning: Success comes in small packages. Read the small print on any contracts and look at details.

ĬNTERPRETATĬON

This is a time of small changes. It is also a time of limitation. It is necessary to combine the changes with the boundaries inflicted. Going too far would be unwise right now.

JUĐGEMENT

> Going with the time leads to success:
> Work on small things, not great things.
> The flying bird brings the message:
> 'Strive not upward; better stay below.'

If you stick at it, you will succeed. However, you must be careful not to overstep the mark. Sometimes it is better to aim for a more readily attainable target.

ĬMAGE

> Thunder on the mountain: loud and near.
> The wise man derives an imperative.

Be true to yourself. Know who you are. Work with time rather than against it. Don't put yourself on too high a pedestal.

LĬNE MEANĬNGS

LĬNE 1

> The fledgling tries to fly too soon.

You have tried too hard too soon and have placed yourself in an

unsafe position. You are not able to meet your responsibilities or maintain your position. You must be careful.

LINE 2

> Seek not to surpass one's master.

If you aim high, you must be prepared to fall short occasionally. You have done well for yourself. Be satisfied with what you have.

LINE 3

> Danger unseen. Take extreme care:
> One may be struck from behind.

People are likely to take advantage of you if you let them. Be careful. Other people aren't necessarily on your side.

LINE 4

> When tempted to take the initiative,
> Be on guard, do not act, be steadfast.

There are problems between you and another. Stay put and don't get too involved. Distance yourself from both them and the problem.

LINE 5

> Dense clouds gather, but still no rain.
> The time of transition is now very near,
> So the prince seeks out the best man.

You have put in for promotion or some form of advancement. You think it is a *fait accompli*, but you are wrong. Another person will win through.

LINE 6

> The bird that flies higher and higher.

Taking advantage of good fortune brings about ill. This is what is happening now. If you continue on the same path and push hard, you will fail. It's up to you.

(63) Chi Chi – Completion

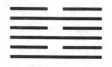

Other keywords: Small continuity/order.

Component trigrams: Fire below, Water above.

Modern meaning: You have achieved much and feel like relaxing. Don't. There are still things which require your attention. Look to reinforce your gains.

Interpretation

This hexagram concerns the peace that one finds in order. It is a time of caution and retaining a happy balance.

Judgement

> Order leads to disorder. Be persevering.
> A time for success, only in small matters.

Remember that things that are sorted can easily become disorganised again. Look at details. Persevere with things and remain cautious.

Image

> Water over fire: a time of perfect order.
> The wise man considers misfortune
> And arms himself against it in advance.

Forearmed is forewarned. If you expect the unexpected, you will never be unprepared. Remember that everything eventually

balances out, and to understand the good times fully, it is necessary to experience the bad occasionally.

Line meanings

Line 1

> One stops in time. No blame.

This is a time of change and of new developments. If you get swept along by things, you may find yourself overstepping the mark. Stay within your limits and within your moral codes.

Line 2

> When trust is withheld,
> Turn inward and wait. Develop within.

You seek recognition which is not forthcoming. Don't do anything. Wait and be patient. Things will change eventually.

Line 3

> An emperor conquers new lands. Danger.

Remember that when looking to expand your ideas, you may tread on a few toes. Be careful.

Line 4

> Even the finest clothes
> Will turn, eventually, to rags.

Problems can crop up at any time. Be prepared for them.

Line 5

> Simplicity is more blessed
> Than much display without warmth.

Don't become conceited, boastful or insincere. This is the danger right now. Look within and be true to yourself.

LINE 6

> After crossing a stream, keep going.
> Turning back is dangerous. Go forward.

There is no point in looking to the past. Move onwards. Things that went wrong can't now be changed, and you must live with the consequences. Keep going, and don't look back.

(64) WEI CHI — BEFORE COMPLETION

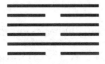

Other keywords: Nearly there/transition.

Component trigrams: Water below, Fire above.

Modern meaning: Wait for the right time before acting, and proceed with caution. There may be things you don't fully appreciate yet. Don't get involved with something you could regret later.

INTERPRETATION

This hexagram is all about change from chaos to order. However, the change is still underway, and things are not yet stable or fixed. This is another cyclical change, as from winter to spring.

JUDGEMENT

> During transition, caution brings success.

> A prick-eared old fox can cross the ice,
> But the rash young fox gets his tail wet.

Being over-confident, naive and inexperienced can and will lead to problems. Likewise, when you think danger is passed is the most vulnerable time.

Image

> Fire and water are opposites by nature,
> So a wise man differentiates with care.
> He separates things in order to unite them,
> That each should find its proper place.

If everything is in its place and in the right order, things will go well. You can't force things together which have no place.

Line meanings

Line 1

> One gets one's tail wet. Humiliation.

Now is not the time to act. You need to be patient and less rash in thinking and action. The time is not yet right.

Line 2

> One holds back. Good. Now be patient.

Still wait. Don't do anything. Prepare for the future but don't put your plans into action.

Line 3

> The time to act has come. Seek helpers.
> To force things brings misfortune.

Don't force the pace. Whilst you should act, it would be better to find people who will help you go in a new direction rather than to continue in the same way and to do it all yourself.

LINE 4

When the struggle comes, be steadfast.

You must act now, and stick to your course. See it through without wavering. You are in the process of creating stability for the future.

LINE 5

The light of the wise man is true.

Things are nearly sorted out. You are involved in new things. This is a new start. You feel more content, and those around you see this.

LINE 6

Drinking the wine in celebration:
But he who wets his head will lose it.

You have finally made it. You can relax and celebrate with others. Be careful, however, that you don't lose sight of your principles by being over-indulgent or falling into the trap of excess.

We have now covered all 64 hexagrams, and can do some practice!

PTER

4 PRACTICE MAKES PERFECT!

We have now covered all the meanings of the trigrams, the hexagrams and the individual lines. We have looked at casting the hexagrams, the methods to use, and what it all means. It is now necessary, before we finish, to make sure we are confident in doing all that we have learned.

Remember, it takes a long time to become proficient in anything, and I Ching is no exception. You must be prepared to make a few mistakes along the way, and must be sure how to cast the hexagram in the first place in order to make full use of the wisdom that I Ching offers.

I suggest that you do several practice throws with the coins or yarrow stalks and draw a few hexagrams, including using moving lines, before even thinking of doing a reading for someone else. Practise with yourself, formulating questions that you need to have answered and make sure you adopt the right frame of mind before undertaking to start.

A TRIAL SAMPLE

Let's pretend that we have done a sample throw. We have come up with hexagram 53 or Chien, which relates to growth. Let's further pretend that lines 2 and 6 are moving lines. Look at the hexagram for Chien again. Put in the moving lines. You will see that this then becomes the hexagram called Ching or The Well, which is number 48. Let's take a look at the individual lines which have changed and then at the whole new hexagram. The question to which we are seeking an answer is 'Should I try for promotion at work?' The person concerned works for a large company and feels that he needs to move on, as the people he is working with do not appreciate his talents and he is capable of doing more with himself. He feels he needs and deserves more responsibility, and ultimately more money.

Chien is all about growth, gradual and slow. It talks about taking things slowly and not moving ahead too quickly. Line 2 suggests that to remain alone would not be a good thing. It is necessary to share things with others, and it would be unwise to turn others away. Line 6 suggests that it is necessary to seek new goals and new challenges. It also suggests that we have the respect of other people.

Looking now at The Well or Ching, we see that the hexagram concerns change. It warns about being sincere and learning about yourself. We further see that line 2 is about using other people for your own ends. Because we are unable to control people as we would wish, we isolate ourselves. It further talks about becoming alienated from people and not showing our good side. Line 6, however, is all about opening up and being more sympathetic to other people. It suggests we try to help others as much as we can.

If you were doing a reading, and got these hexagrams and moving lines, how would you interpret the answer? Remember there isn't necessarily a totally wrong or totally right answer here.

In the original hexagram, line 2 is about sharing things and not turning others away. We have moved from this to be told that we have wanted to control others, and so have isolated ourselves, become alienated from other people. Can you see how these two match up? The message is clear. We are being self-centred. We are only alone because we have failed to manipulate other people. We are therefore learning the reasons for our exile from 'the group'.

In line 6 of the original hexagram, we are told that we have a new goal, things are going well and we have the respect of other people. In the next hexagram, however, we are told that learning is all well and good, but there is also spiritual learning to be undertaken. We are told that we must be sympathetic to other people and help as much as we can. Again, can you see how these two lines marry together?

Looking at moving lines is all about learning how one situation changes into another, or how the two interrelate so we learn more about the existing situation.

So then, we have looked at the two lines. We have looked at each full hexagram. What are we learning here? Have we received the correct answer to our original question. If you were advising the person concerned, would you suggest that he seeks promotion or not, and what further input would you give on the situation? If I were doing the reading, I would suggest that he seeks promotion, but consider adopting a different attitude to those around him. Would you say the same thing?

As I said at the outset, I Ching gives answers on which one can meditate. It is all about change. If we are to change for the better, we can, in my opinion, do no better than consulting such a source of wisdom. Ultimately, however, it is up to us whether we choose to change, take up the advice given, or not. Remember, if you are doing a reading for someone, you can't make their minds up for them; that is their privilege and prerogative.

There are many times in your life when you might need some guidance and advice. You may choose many forms of help, esoteric or otherwise. You may end up feeling totally confused. The thing to remember when consulting I Ching is that you are given straight answers. You can also be given situations where change is indicated, as with moving lines. From that information, you can then move forward. Rather than being given a set path to follow, you can then be given a direction, leaving you to choose the path.

There is much more information that could be given about I Ching, but maybe that is better left until you have mastered the basics. At the end of this book, you will find a reading list. This is not exhaustive but could provide you with further avenues of investigation.

If you are seeking to develop your self-awareness, and feel you have only just started on the road to discovery, I Ching will give you a vehicle with which to move forward. It will not, however, reveal the ultimate destination, for that remains the unknown factor, which may take many lifetimes to discover and understand. Remember, always, to be true to yourself and your fellow man. Accept responsibility for your actions. Be sympathetic, honest, true and genuine. Once you achieve this state of mind, you will be on your way to becoming what I Ching calls a 'superior man' (or woman).

fURThER READING

Craze, Richard, *Feng Shui for Beginners*, Headway, 1994

Fox, Judy, Hughes, Karen, and Tampion, John, *An Illuminated I Ching*, Neville Spearman, England, 1983

Knight, C. Damian, *The I Ching on Business and Decision Making*, Rider, England, 1987

Markert, Christopher, *I Ching, the No. 1 Success Formula*, Aquarian Press, 1987

Palmer, Martin, Kwok Man Ho and O'Brien, Joanne, *The Fortune Teller's I Ching*, Rider, England, 1987

Walker, Barbara G., *The I Ching of the Goddess*, Harper & Row, England, 1987

Wing, R.L., *The Illustrated I Ching*, Aquarian Press, England, 1987